MW01148065

SPANISH WORKBOOK FOR ADULTS

Quick Start Guide for Busy People with Fun Activities, Interactive Exercises, and Easy-to-Follow Lessons for Absolute Beginners

MORELINGUA ACADEMY

© Copyright MORELINGUA ACADEMY 2024

All rights reserved

The content within this book may not be reproduced, duplicated, or transmitted without direct written permission from the author or the publisher.

Under no circumstances will any blame or legal responsibility be held against the publisher, or author, for any damages, reparation, or monetary loss due to the information contained within this book. Either directly or indirectly. You are responsible for your own choices, actions, and results.

Legal Notice:

This book is copyright-protected. This book is only for personal use. You cannot amend, distribute, sell, use, quote, or paraphrase any part, of the content within this book, without the consent of the author or publisher.

Disclaimer Notice:

Please note the information contained within this document is for educational and entertainment purposes only. All effort has been expended to present accurate, up-to-date, and reliable, complete information. No warranties of any kind are declared or implied. Readers acknowledge that the author is not engaging in the rendering of legal, financial, medical, or professional advice. The content within this book has been derived from various sources. Please consult a licensed professional before attempting any techniques outlined in this book.

By reading this document, the reader agrees that under no circumstances is the author responsible for any losses, direct or indirect, which are incurred as a result of the use of the information contained within this document, including, but not limited to, — errors, omissions, or inaccuracies.

ii

TABLE OF CONTENTS

Morelingua Academy

INTRODUCTION

E ver found yourself sitting at a café, overhearing a lively conversation in Spanish beside you, and thought, "I wish I could jump in"? Or perhaps you've been on the brink of ordering food in a quaint Spanish town, only to resort to pointing and awkward smiles because, let's face it, "dos cervezas, por favor" is the extent of your Spanish repertoire. Trust me, you're not alone. The journey of learning Spanish as an adult is often paved with good intentions, a sprinkle of embarrassment, and a healthy dose of frustration.

Hey there! I'm the person behind this labor of love—a workbook that's about to become your new best friend on your Spanish learning adventure. Once upon a time, I was in your shoes. The shoes of fumbling through basic greetings, mixing up my "por" and "para," and feeling like I'd never get past "¿Cómo estás?". But, as someone who's tackled those same challenges head-on, found ways to not just learn but love Spanish, and developed a unique method to pass on the joy of language learning, I'm here to tell you: there's hope. And it's packed into the pages of this book.

This isn't your average, run-of-the-mill language guide. Oh no. This is a comprehensive yet utterly approachable workbook designed with you—the absolute beginner, the adult learner—in mind. I've filled it with practical exercises, cultural tidbits, and innovative techniques that cater to how adults learn best. Plus, there's a sprinkle of humor because, let's be honest, laughing at ourselves is half the fun of learning something new.

The vision? To demolish those language barriers brick by brick, empowering you to confidently stride into the Spanish-speaking world, ready to chat, joke, and maybe even dream in Spanish. Through a structured program, each week builds upon the last, guiding you from a hesitant beginner to an enthusiastic, capable speaker. By the end of our journey together, not only will you have a solid foundation in Spanish, but you'll also possess the tools and gumption to keep exploring the language on your terms.

But wait, there's more! This book is jam-packed with diverse learning materials to suit every style—think audio recordings to perfect your pronunciation, interactive exercises to finesse your grammar, cultural anecdotes to enrich your understanding, and practical dialogues to boost your conversational chops. It's all about providing a holistic, well-rounded learning experience.

Now, let's talk tone. This book gets you. It knows the fear of making mistakes, the dread of feeling silly. That's why every page is drenched in support, encouragement, and a bit of that friendly nudge to remind you that mistakes aren't just okay—they're crucial to your growth. So, breathe easy, laugh off the hiccups, and keep pushing forward.

I also want to urge you to stretch beyond these pages. Engage with Spanish-speaking folks, whether that's by joining a local language meetup, making a Spanish-speaking friend, or diving into online communities. Real-world practice is the golden ticket to bringing your new skills to life.

As we stand at the starting line of this journey, I'm throwing down the gauntlet. Embrace this challenge, immerse yourself in the vibrant tapestry of Spanish language and culture, and I promise, you'll emerge not just with a new skill set, but with a richer, more colorful perspective on the world.

Ready? ¡Vamos!

Your guide, cheerleader, and fellow language enthusiast.

CHAPTER 1

GOOD MORNING AND GOODBYE

1. Cultural Theme: A Friendly Culture

Spanish-speaking people from Spain or Latin America are known to be warm and gregarious. And it's true. They have fewer formalities when establishing relationships with others, and you will always feel welcome when you travel to their countries. For example, if you meet someone in Perú or Argentina, they might invite you to dinner at their home that same day without much ado. Spanish and Latin American people have a carefree attitude and a flexible mindset that helps them take things in stride. So if you stop someone on the street asking for directions, they will immediately try to help you get to your destination without worrying about the time it's taking away from whatever activity they were on their way to doing. That is why we consider it essential to start this Spanish Workbook with a way to greet and take leave of friends and formal relationships. Because if you travel to a Spanish-speaking country, you will definitely need to know these expressions!

2. Vocabulary

Greetings and Polite Expressions

> You will notice in Spanish we include quotation and exclamation marks both at the beginning and at the end of the sentence.

Hi	Hola
Good morning	Buenos días
Good afternoon	Buenas tardes
Good night/Good evening	Buenas noches
How are things?	¿Qué tal?
How are you?	¿Cómo estás? (informal) or ¿Cómo está? (formal)
Very well, and you?	Muy bien, ¿y tú? (informal) or Muy bien, ¿y usted? (formal)
So-so	Regular/Más o menos
I'm glad to hear it	Me alegro
A pleasure to meet you	Mucho gusto
A pleasure to meet you too	Mucho gusto/Encantado/a
Goodbye	Adiós
See you later	Hasta luego
See you tomorrow	Hasta mañana
See you soon	Hasta pronto

Best wishes for everyday life

Have a good day	Te deseo un buen día (informal) Le deseo un buen día (formal)
Have a great weekend	Que tengas un gran fin de semana (informal) Que tenga un gran fin de semana (formal)
Very best wishes	Muchos saludos
Good luck	Mucha suerte
All the best to you	Lo mejor para ti (informal) Lo mejor para usted (formal)
I hope to see you again	Espero volver a verte (informal) Espero volver a verlo (formal)

Season's greetings

Merry Christmas and a Happy New Year	Feliz Navidad y próspero año nuevo
Happy Easter	Feliz Pascua
Happy Christmas to you all	Felices fiestas a todos

Birthdays

Happy Birthday!	¡Feliz cumpleaños!
Happy Anniversary!	¡Feliz aniversario!

Wishing someone well

Get well soon	Que te mejores pronto (informal)
	Que se mejore pronto (formal)
Good luck!	¡Suerte!
I hope everything goes well	Espero que todo salga bien
Good luck with the exam	¡Suerte en el examen!
Have a great trip	Buen viaje

Congratulations

Congratulations!	¡Felicitaciones!
Wishing you the best!	¡Muchas felicidades!

Polite expressions

Thank you	Gracias
Thank you very much	Muchas gracias
You're welcome	De nada
Please	Por favor
I'm sorry, excuse me, pardon me	Perdón, disculpe (you can also use these words to get someone's attention, like at a restaurant).
Pardon me, excuse me	Permiso (when you ask for permission to pass by or through a group of people).

Dialogue

Informal situation

María: Hola, Juan, ¿qué tal?

Juan: Muy bien, ¿y tú?

María: Muy bien. Hasta mañana.

Juan: Adiós.

Formal situation

Señor Pérez: Buenos días, señor Ocampo.

Señor Ocampo: Buenos días, señor Pérez. ¿Cómo está usted?

Señor Pérez: Bien, gracias, ¿y usted?

Señor Ocampo: Bien, gracias. Hasta luego.

Señor Pérez: Adiós.

In English we use the **you** pronoun for both formal and informal situations. Spanish has two different words for **you** (singular): **tú** and **usted**. **Tú** implies a familiar relationship, like your friends or relatives. **Usted** is used with people whom you call by their title and last name (Sr. Pérez).

As for the plural, English still uses the same pronoun: **you**. Spanish uses **ustedes** as a plural for **tú** and **ustedes** in Latin America. In Spain, however, the plural of **tú** is **vosotros/vosotras**.

Let's practice

A. Write what you would say after the following greetings:

1. Hola _____

2. ¿Cómo estás? _____

3. ¿Qué tal? _____

4. Buenas noches _____

5. Hasta mañana _____

6. Muchas gracias _____

7. Adiós _____

8. Buenos días _____

9. Mucho gusto _____

10. Buenas tardes _____

B. What would you say in each situation?

1. It's Christmas day, and you meet a friend:

   _____

2. You're trying to get through a group of people on the train to get off _____

3. You're in a restaurant trying to get the waiter's attention _____

4. It's 3:00 p.m., and you run into a friend

   _____

5. It's 10:00 a.m., and you're entering your class

   _____

6. It's 8:00 p.m., and you're stepping into a restaurant

   _____

7. You're on a crowded bus and must find your way out because you're leaving at the next stop _____

8. Someone gives you her seat on the train _____

9. You accidentally step on someone's foot in a line
_____

10. Someone thanks you for a present _____

C. Complete these dialogues: one is informal (with a friend), and the other is between two acquaintances.

1. Pedro: Hola, Luis, _____

   Luis: _____

   Pedro: _____

   Luis: Me alegro. Hasta pronto.

   Pedro: _____

2. Señor Alonso: Buenas tardes, señor Ortiz

   Señor Ortiz: _____, señor Alonso. ¿_____ usted?

   Señor Alonso: _____, gracias, ¿y _____?

   Señor Ortiz: Bien, _____. Hasta pronto.

   Señor Pérez: _____.

D. What would you say...

1. When you find out a friend is sick:

   _____

2. When you want to wish someone a great trip:

   _____

3. When you want to wish Happy Easter to someone:

   _____

4. When you want to congratulate someone:

   _____

5. When you want to wish a friend, everything goes well:

   _____

6. When you want to wish a friend a happy anniversary:

   _____

7. When you want to wish a friend he does well in an exam:

   _____

8. When you want to wish someone a happy birthday:

   _____

9. When a friend lets you know she's getting married:

   _____

10. When your friend tells you he's being operated on:

   _____

3. Reading comprehension of cultural theme

Since friendship is essential in Latin America, we included a poem on this theme by Cuban poet José Martí (1853-1895). This poem is about the need to care for friends who are sincere and loyal to us but also for those who might harm us. The poet grows a white rose to offer it to a faithful friend. But he also provides one to those who aren't as loyal. The idea is to extend kindness to everyone, even those who might hurt us. There is no point in harboring resentment towards anyone. You will find the translation right next to each Spanish line. Don't worry if you can't understand the Spanish structures yet; this is just a way to ease you into the language and start understanding how it works.

Cultivo una rosa blanca, de José Martí	I Grow a White Rose, by José Martí
Cultivo una rosa blanca	I grow a white rose
en junio como en enero,	in June, as in January
para el amigo sincero	for the sincere friend
que me da su mano franca.	who gives me his frank hand.
Y para el vil que me arranca	And for the vile one who tears away from me
el corazón con que vivo	the heart with which I live
cardo ni espina cultivo,	thistle nor thorn I grow,
cultivo una rosa blanca	I grow a white rose.

Let's Practice

A. Try to match the following Spanish words from the poem with their meaning in English. You'll probably recognize many of them because their spelling is similar or because you've come across them in different media. Remember, this is your first lesson, and mistakes are okay!

Blanca	rose
cardo	thorn
cultivo	hand
vil	white
junio	grow
mano	January
Espina	sincere
amigo	thistle
sincero	heart
enero	June
Rosa	vile
corazón	friend

B. Can you guess what these verbs mean?

cultivo (from the verb "cultivar")_____

da (from the verb "dar")_____

arranca (from the verb "arrancar") _____

vivo (from the verb "vivir")_____

4. Grammar concept: The Alphabet

The Spanish alphabet (el *alfabeto*) has twenty-seven letters. Three letters — **ch, ll, rr** — called *digraphs,* used to belong in the Spanish alphabet, but the Royal Spanish Academy no longer treats them as letters in their own right. However, they are still very much used in Spanish. As for the ñ, it is a separate letter and does belong in the Spanish alphabet. The letters **k** and **w** only appear in words borrowed from other languages. The following table explains the pronunciation of letters different from their English counterparts.

LETTERS	NAMES OF LETTERS	PRONOUNCED	EXAMPLES
a	a	Like the *a* in *father*	*Argentina*
b	be	The *b* sound is somewhere between the *b* and the *v*: a fuzzy, bland sound.	*Bolivia*
c	ce	ce, ci: [s] sound ca, co, cu: [k] sound	*Cecilia* *Colombia*
d	de	Same as in English	*Diana*
e	e	Like the *e* in *men*	*Ecuador*
f	efe	Same as in English	*Finlandia*
g	ge	Ga, go, gu: [g] sound Ge, gi: like Spanish *j* or the strong English *h*	*Guatemala* *Gibraltar*
h	hache	Always mute! Do *not* pronounce it like the *j* in jalapeño!	*Honduras*
i	i	Like the *i* in machine	*Ibiza*
j	jota	Like the English *h,* but with more force. It's almost like gargling!	*Japón*

k	ka	Same as in English	Kansas
l	ele	Same as in English	Londres
m	eme	Same as in English	México
n	ene	Same as in English	Noruega
ñ	eñe	Like the *ny* sound in *canyon*	España
o	o	Like the *o* sound in *top* but shorter	Oslo
p	pe	Same as the unaspirated English *p* in *spell*. Make sure there is no puff of air like with the English *p*	Portugal
q	cu	The Spanish *q* is always followed by *u* (which remains silent) and used with vowels *e* and *i*: *que* and *qui*. It is pronounced like the *k* sound in *cake*.	Quito
r	ere	At the beginning of a word pronounced like a trilled *r*: *Rumania* In the middle of a word, pronounced softly, like the English *tt* in the word *butter*: *Perú*.	Río de Janeiro Cartagena
s	ese	Same as in English	Sevilla
t	te	Same as in English but make sure there is no puff of air	Puerto Rico

u	u	Like the *u* in *rule*, but short.	Port*u*gal
v	ve	Same sound as the *b*, a soft version of the English *b*.	*V*enezuela
w	doble v	Same as in English	*W*ashington
x	equis	Same as in English or like the Spanish *j* (México, Texas)	Te*x*as
y	i griega	Like *i* in some countries (Peru) and like *sh* in others (Argentina)	*Y*akarta
z	ceta	Like the English letter *s*. Same sound as the Spanish *s*	*Z*aragoza

Spanish digraphs

ch	che	Like the *ch* in English *cheese*	*Ch*ile
ll	elle	Like *y* in *yes* (in Spain and some Latin American countries like Peru) or like the *s* in *measure* in countries like Argentina and Uruguay.	Sevi*ll*a
rr	erre	A trilled sound, like several *r*'s in a row	Ma*rr*uecos

In Spanish the word *y* (and) sounds like the letter *i*.

Pronunciation Points

The Spanish language boasts five vowels: A, E, I, O, and U. Each one is pronounced in a clear, distinct manner that remains consistent regardless of the word they're in. This consistency starkly contrasts English, where vowels can have multiple sounds, making pronunciation a guessing game for learners. In Spanish, the vowel 'A' is consistently pronounced in 'father,' 'E' as in 'pet,' 'I' as in 'machine,' 'O' as in 'torn,' and 'U' as in 'rude.' This uniformity ensures that once you master the sounds of these five vowels, you can pronounce any Spanish word with greater ease and accuracy. The good news is that words are pronounced exactly as they are written. As you practice and become more familiar with these sounds, your natural hesitation to pronounce new words will diminish, and your ability to speak with confidence will grow.

In Spanish, the letter k is used only in words that have their origin in foreign languages. For example, *kilo* and *kilometer*.

For example, consider the word "agua" (water). Regardless of its position in a sentence, the pronunciation of the vowels remains unchanged, offering a

The rolling *r* is the hallmark of the Spanish language, a sound that vibrates through conversations and adds a musical quality to the spoken word. It's produced by lightly tapping the tip of your tongue against the roof of your mouth, right behind your front teeth, similar to the way you'd pronounce a soft *d* in English. For many, this sound is a bit of a gymnastic feat for the tongue, but fear not—practice makes perfect.

predictability that is comforting to new learners. This reliability forms the bedrock of your pronunciation skills, providing a solid foundation to explore the broader aspects of the Spanish language.

Pronunciation Practice

It's tricky to practice pronunciation by yourself, but everything is possible. Utilize online pronunciation guides and resources specifically designed for language learners. Websites like Forvo provide audio recordings of words pronounced by native speakers. Use the exercises below to practice pronouncing words, and listen to the native version to improve your pronunciation.

A. A simple yet effective practice is to recite the vowels aloud, paying close attention to the shape of your mouth and the placement of your tongue. This physical awareness is crucial for reproducing the sounds accurately.

a - e - i - o - u

B. Pronounce these names, focusing on the vowel sounds, and listen to the correct version on your computer to compare and improve your pronunciation.

Marta - Pedro - Ignacio - Mónica - Raúl - Teresa - Pilar - Martín - Isabel - Alicia

C. Pronounce these place names and listen to the correct version on your computer to compare and improve your pronunciation.

Nevada - Nueva York - España - Turquía - Rusia - Chile - Sicilia - Suecia - Inglaterra - Toronto - Rumania - Checoslovaquia - Portugal - Bélgica - Sierra Nevada - Mozambique

D. Spell these U.S. place names in Spanish. All of them are of Hispanic origin:

El Paso - El Álamo - Laredo - Montana - Colorado - San Francisco - Las Vegas - Amarillo - Los Ángeles.

E. Combine the 'B' sound with each vowel, then the 'R' sound, then the 'C' sound, then the 'G' sound, then the 'H' sound and finally the 'J' sound:

ba - be - bi - bo - bu

ra - re - ri - ro - ru

ca - ce - ci - co - cu

ga - ge - gi - go - gu

ha - he - hi - ho - hu

ja - je - ji - jo - ju

F. Now let's mix syllables, being careful to pronounce each vowel with a short sound:

1. pa fa la ma ta	6. po fo lo mo to
2. pe fe le me te	7. pu fu lu mu tu
3. pi fi li me ti	8. so la te mi su

G. Practicing the middle r: try saying words with an r in the middle, like:

pero (but) - cara (expensive) - pura (pure) - mira (look) - toro (bull) - pera (pear) - faro (lighthouse) - cura (cure) - corazón (heart) - para (stop)

H. Now ramp it up: challenge yourself with words that start with **r** (remember to roll your tongue!):

rojo (red) - real (real) - río (river) - ruta (route) - rana (frog) - ratón (mouse) - rosa (rose) - rama (branch) - rayo (beam)

I. Try saying this tongue twister designed to make your tongue dance:

Erre con erre cigarro	R with R is a cigar
Erre con erre barril,	R with R is a barrel
rápido corren los carros,	the cars run fast
cargados en el ferrocarril	loaded on the railway

J. Try saying these words that start with *h*. Remember, the *h* is silent!

hola (hi) - helado (ice cream) - hacer (to do/make) - hambre (hunger) - hada (fairy) - hora (time) - hoja (leaf) - higo (fig) - hilo (thread) - hijo (son)

K. Match the Spanish spelling with its corresponding description.

1. **V**   a. never pronounced

2. **r** at the beginning of a   b. like the *g* in Engish go or **rr**
   word   in the middle of a word

3.	ñ		c. like *ch* in English *chair*
4.	**g** before **e** or **i**; also **j**		ch. similar to the *ny* sound in *canyon*
5.	**ch**		d. a trilled sound
6.	**g** before **a, o,** or **u**		e. pronounced softly, like the English *tt* in the word *butter*.
7.	**Ll**		f. like Spanish *j* or the strong English *h*.
8.	**r** in the middle of the word		g. like the Spanish *b*.
9.	**h**		h. like *y* in *yes* or the *s* in measure.

5. Communication Tips

This section will focus on typical situations you may encounter when traveling to Spanish-speaking countries. Learning a new language to use in your travels is one of the best reasons to do so, wherever your journey takes you. Traveling to a new country opens you up to adventure, and what better way to immerse yourself fully than to go on your voyage with your language skills in hand? There are actually 21 countries that state Spanish as their official language: Spain, Mexico, Costa Rica, El Salvador, Guatemala, Honduras, Nicaragua, Panama, Cuba, Dominican Republic, Puerto Rico, Argentina, Bolivia, Chile, Colombia, Ecuador, Paraguay, Peru, Uruguay, Venezuela, and Equatorial Guinea. So pick the one that appeals to you, board your plane, and prepare to practice your Spanish!

At the airport immigration desk

Your first stop before entering a new country is the airport immigration desk. The following is a typical exchange you might experience before an immigration officer in your Spanish-speaking destination country.

Immigration officer: —Buenas noches, señorita.	—Good evening, Miss.
Immigration officer: —¿De dónde viene?	—¿Where are you arriving from?
Passenger: —De los Estados Unidos.	—From the U.S.
Immigration officer: —Pasaporte, por favor.	—Passport, please.
Passenger: —Aquí tiene mi pasaporte.	—Here is my passport.
Immigration officer: —¿En qué vuelo llegó?	—What flight did you arrive in?
Passenger: —En American Airlines 1350.	—On American Airlines 1350.
Immigration officer: —¿De qué nacionalidad es?	—What nationality are you?
Passenger: —Soy estadounidense.	—I'm from the U.S.
Immigration officer: —¿Cuánto tiempo estará en el país?	

	—How long are you staying in the country?
Passenger: —Diez días.	—Ten days.
Immigration officer: —¿Viaja por placer o por trabajo?	—Are you traveling for pleasure or work?
Passenger: —Viajo por placer.	—I'm traveling for pleasure.
Immigration officer: —¿En dónde se aloja?	—Where are you staying?
Passenger: —En el Hotel Mariott.	—At the Mariott hotel.
Immigration officer: —Disfrute de su estadía.	—Enjoy your stay.
Passenger: —Gracias.	—Thank you.

Vocabulary

- vuelo: flight

- estadía: stay

- mostrador de inmigración: immigration desk

- declarar: to declare

- la aduana: customs

- el extranjero: abroad

- la inmigración: immigration

- inmigrante: immigrant

- emigrar: to emigrate

- la nacionalidad: nationality

- el pasaporte: passport

- la planilla: form

- el/la viajero/a: traveler

Practice repeating these words and comparing your pronunciation to the one you hear on any dedicated website like SpanishDictionary.com.

6. Answer Key

2.

A.

1. Hola/Buenos días/Buenas tardes/Buenas noches

2. Bien, ¿y tú?/Bien, ¿y usted?

3. Muy bien, gracias, ¿y tú?/Muy bien, gracias, ¿y usted?

4. Buenas noches/Adiós/Hasta mañana

5. Adiós/Hasta mañana

6. De nada

7. Hasta luego/Adiós

8. Buenos días/Hola/¿Qué tal?

9. Muchos gusto/Encantado/a

10. Buenas tardes/Hola

B.

1. ¡Feliz Navidad!

2. Permiso, por favor/Disculpe

3. Perdón/Disculpe

4. Buenas tardes

5. Buenos días

6. Buenas noches

7. Permiso, por favor

8. Gracias

9. Perdón

10. De nada

C.

1. Pedro: Hola, Luis, ¿cómo estás?

   Luis: Bien, ¿y tú?

   Pedro: Muy bien, gracias.

   Luis: Me alegro. Hasta pronto.

   Pedro: Adiós.

2. Señor Alonso: Buenas tardes, señor Ortiz.

Señor Ortiz: <u>Buenas tardes</u>, señor Alonso. <u>¿Cómo está</u> usted?

Señor Alonso: <u>Muy bien</u>, gracias, <u>¿y usted?</u>

Señor Ortiz: Bien, <u>gracias</u>. Hasta pronto.

Señor Pérez: <u>Hasta luego </u>or <u>Adiós.</u>

D.

1. Que te mejores pronto.
2. Buen viaje.
3. Feliz Pascua.
4. Felicitaciones.
5. Espero que todo salga bien.
6. ¡Feliz aniversario!
7. Suerte en el examen/Espero que todo salga bien.
8. ¡Feliz cumpleaños!
9. Muchas felicidades.
10. Espero que todo salga bien.

3.

A. Matching pairs:

blanca-white	cardo-thistle	cultivo-grow	vil-vile
junio-June	mano-hand	espina-thorn	amigo-friend
sincero-sincere	enero-January	rosa-rose	corazón-heart

B. cultivo: grow

da: give

arranca: tears away

vivo: live

4.

J.

1. g: like the Spanish b.
2. d: a trilled sound.
3. ch: similar to the *ny* sound in *canyon.*
4. f: like Spanish *j* or the strong English *h.*
5. c: like *ch* in the English *chair.*
6. b: like the *g* in English *go.*
7. h: like *y* in yes or the *s* in measure.
8. e: pronounced softly, like the English *tt* in the word *butter.*
9. a: never pronounced.

CHAPTER 2

THE WORLD AROUND US

1. Cultural Theme: Getting around

While foreigners may think Spanish-speaking countries are all the same, the truth of the matter is they have only one thing in common: the language. That said, there is already a vast difference between Spain and countries in Latin America, and these, in turn, have their own unique flavor. On the one hand, Spain is a developed country with a high-income economy and advanced infrastructure; on the other, Latin American countries vary widely in terms of economic development. Likewise, Spain is a diverse country with distinct regional cultures, and Latin America also has a hugely diverse culture with a rich mix of indigenous, African, and European influences. Though each Spanish-speaking country has its unique culture, some cultural aspects are common across geographic boundaries. Walking around any of the world's Spanish-speaking cities, you may feel a historic colonial-era vibe in their city centers, similar to what you feel when visiting Spanish towns. That is because Spain and Portugal colonized Latin American countries during the 16th to 19th centuries, shaping their culture and architecture. Of course, due to societal, technological, and cultural changes that occurred during the late 19th and 20th centuries, the major cities in Latin America have acquired the modern trappings of contemporary life, with urban amenities and efficient public transportation networks connecting different city areas. If you travel to a Spanish-speaking country, you should feel confident about asking for directions and finding your way around the neighborhood where you're staying. It's also good to know vocabulary about streets and traffic. Dive into this chapter to learn about it and avoid getting lost in your next destination!

> Notice **derecho** (straight) is not the same as **derecha** (right). You say **Camine derecho** (walk straight), but **Doble a la derecha** (Turn right).

2. Vocabulary

Asking for Directions

Terms

North	Norte
Sur	South
West	Oeste
East	Este
Close by	Cerca
Far away	Lejos
Desde	From
Toward	Hacia
In front of	En frente de

Between	Entre
Behind	Detrás
Straight	Derecho
Left	Izquierda
Right	Derecha
To the right of	A la derecha de
To the left of	A la izquierda de
A mano derecha	To the right
A mano izquierda	To the left
The first	La primera
The second	La segunda
The third	La tercera
Public transport	Transporte público
Block	Cuadra
One block	Una cuadra
Two blocks	Dos cuadras
Ten blocks	Diez cuadras
Twenty blocks	Veinte cuadras
Street	Calle
Road	Carretera
Avenue	Avenida
Sidewalk	Acera
Highway	Autopista
Park	Parque
Tunnel	Túnel

Traffic lights	Semáforo
Sign	Señal
Traffic circle	Rotonda
Crossroads	Intersección
Bus stop	Parada de autobús
Train station	Estación de tren
Pedestrian crossing	Paso peatonal
Parking	Estacionamiento

The verb **tomar** has three meanings in Spanish.

To drink: **tomo** un vaso de agua (I drink a glass of water)

To grab: **tomo** una piedra (I grab a rock)

To take a means of transport: **tomo** un avión (I take an airplane)

Verbs and phrases

We've used the **usted** verb form (the formal second-person singular pronoun) because when you're traveling and asking for directions, it's usually a stranger you're talking to.

Even though we haven't started talking about verbs yet, we're using several verbs here in the formal second-person singular (usted) to give directions. These verbs are: **siga** (from **seguir**, which means **go straight ahead** or **go on**), **camine** (from **caminar**, which means **walk**), **cruce** (from **cruzar**, which means **cross**), **doble** (from **doblar**, which means **turn** or **take**), **pase** (from **pasar**, which means **go past**), **tome** (from **tomar**, which means **take**), **pase por** (from **pasar por**, which means **go through**).

Go on this road	Siga por esta calle
Go straight on/ahead	Siga derecho
Walk straight on	Camine derecho
Cruce la calle	Cross the street
It's ____ blocks away	Está a ____ cuadras
Walk	Camine
Take	Doble
Go through the tunnel	Pase por el túnel
It's on your left/right	Está a la izquierda/derecha
Take a right	Doble a la derecha
Take a left	Doble a la izquierda
Take the first right	Doble a la derecha en la primera
Take the second left	Doble a la izquierda en la segunda
Take the bus	Tome el autobús
Take the train or the metro	Tome el tren o el metro
Travel by boat	Tome un barco
Travel by plane	Tome un avión
Travel by foot	Camine
Travel by taxi	Tome un taxi
Turn	Doblar
Cross	Cruce
Turn to the right	Doble a la derecha
Turn to the left	Doble a la izquierda
Pass by	Pase por

Go through	Pase por
Go past (a place)	Pase (el lugar)
Go along	Siga por
Take an exit	Tome la salida

Dialogue I

Let's pretend you're a tourist and want to visit a museum in the Spanish-speaking country you are visiting. This is your first time in this city. You leave your hotel, walk a few blocks, and suddenly don't know how to go. You're completely lost! You stop someone on the street to get directions. Remember when doing so to be polite and use your **por favor, gracias, permiso,** and **disculpe** words. You can also use your hands to indicate where you want to go.

Tourist: Disculpe, señor, ¿me puede ayudar?	Excuse me, sir, can you help me?
Local: Claro.	Of course.
Tourist: ¿Hay un museo cerca de acá?	Is there a museum close by?
Local: Sí, hay un museo cerca de acá.	Yes, there's a museum close by.
Tourist: Por favor, ¿puede indicarme cómo llegar al museo desde acá?	Please, can you tell me how to get to the museum from here?
Local: Por supuesto	Of course.
Tourist: ¿Está muy lejos?	Is it too far away?

Local: No, está muy cerca.	No, it's very near.
Tourist: ¿A cuántas cuadras está?	How many blocks is it from here?
Local: Está a diez cuadras.	It's ten blocks from here.
Tourist: Disculpe, puede repetir?	Sorry, could you please repeat that?
Local: Sí, el museo está a diez cuadras de acá.	Yes, the museum is ten blocks from here.
Tourist: ¿Qué autobús me lleva al museo?	What bus takes me to the museum?
Local: El autobús número 35.	Bus number 35.
Tourist: ¿Dónde está la parada, por favor?	Where is the bus stop, please?
Local: Está a cinco cuadras de acá.	It's five blocks from here.
Tourist: Entonces, iré a pie hasta allá.	So I'll walk there.
Local: Sí, no está muy lejos.	Yes, it's not very far.
Tourist: Muchas gracias.	Thank you very much.
Local: De nada.	You're welcome.

Dialogue II

You're in your car and stop a local woman to ask her for directions to a restaurant.

Tourist: Perdón, señorita, ¿puede ayudarme?	Excuse me, miss, ¿can you help me?
Local: Sí, claro.	Yes, of course.
Tourist: ¿Dónde hay un restaurante cerca?	Where is there a restaurant near here?
Local: Hay uno a veinte cuadras.	There is one twenty blocks from here.
Tourist: ¿Cómo llego?	How do I get there?
Local: Siga por esta calle hasta llegar el semáforo.	Go straight on this street until you get to the street light.
Tourist: ¿Y luego?	And then?
Local: Pase por un parque.	Go past a park.
Local: Y siga derecho	And go straight.
Local: Luego pase a través de un túnel.	Go through a tunnel.
Local: Y doble a la izquierda.	And turn left.
Local: El restaurante está en la primera cuadra, a la derecha.	The restaurant is on the first block, to the right.
Turista: Muchas gracias, señorita.	Thank you very much, miss.
Local: De nada.	You're welcome.

Dialogue III

You're in a city and need to get to the train station. This is how you would ask for directions:

Tourist: Disculpe, señor, ¿dónde está la estación de tren?	Excuse me, sir, where is the train station?
Local: Está a tres cuadras de acá.	It's three blocks from here.
Tourist: ¿Cómo llego?	How do I get there?
Local: Camine derecho dos cuadras. Luego, doble a la derecha y camine 1 cuadra más. La estación de tren está en frente del parque.	Walk straight on two blocks. Then turn right and walk one more block. The train station is in front of the park.
Tourist: Muchas gracias.	Thank you very much.
Local: De nada.	You're welcome.
Tourist: Adiós.	Goodbye.

Let's practice

A. Using the vocabulary list above and the box on your right with tourist attractions you might visit on a trip, join the expressions on the left with their matching equivalent:

Places to visit when you travel

museum: museo
restaurant: restaurante
park: parque
library: biblioteca
hotel: hotel
bar: bar
shopping mall: centro comercial
cathedral: catedral
farmacia: drugstore
bank: banco
hospital: hospital

Doble a la izquierda	Go past the library
Tome la salida 4	Take a left
Siga por esta calle	It's on your right
Tome el tren	Walk straight on
El teatro está a una cuadra	Go straight on
Cruce el paso peatonal	The theater is one block away
Pase la biblioteca	Go straight on this road
La catedral está a dos cuadras	Take the train
Camine derecho	Take exit 4
Está a la derecha	The cathedral is two blocks away
Siga derecho	Cross the pedestrian crossing

B. Fill in the blanks with the right verb:

a. _____ derecho.	b. _____ por el túnel	c. _____ a la izquierda.
d. _____ en taxi.	e. _____ a la izquierda.	f. _____ por la biblioteca.
g. _____ a la derecha	h. _____ un avión.	i. _____ un taxi.

C. ¿Where do they take you? Look at the grid below and follow the directions to see where they lead you.

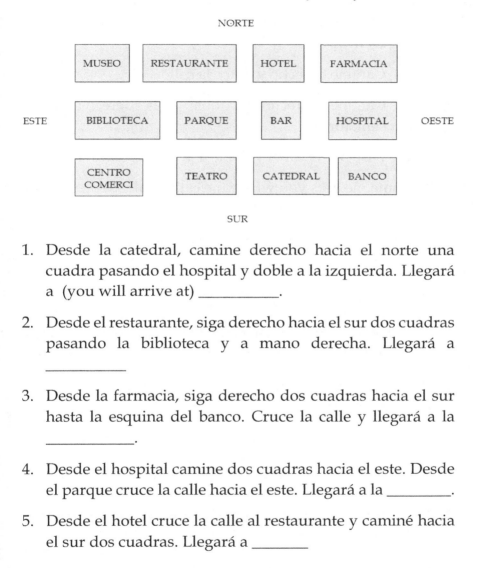

1. Desde la catedral, camine derecho hacia el norte una cuadra pasando el hospital y doble a la izquierda. Llegará a (you will arrive at) _____.

2. Desde el restaurante, siga derecho hacia el sur dos cuadras pasando la biblioteca y a mano derecha. Llegará a

    _____

3. Desde la farmacia, siga derecho dos cuadras hacia el sur hasta la esquina del banco. Cruce la calle y llegará a la

    _____.

4. Desde el hospital camine dos cuadras hacia el este. Desde el parque cruce la calle hacia el este. Llegará a la _____.

5. Desde el hotel cruce la calle al restaurante y caminé hacia el sur dos cuadras. Llegará a _____

D. Pick the correct answer according to each question.

1. Someone asks you for directions to get to the park. You need to tell them to walk straight on and take a right at the traffic lights.

   a. Camine derecho y cruce la calle.

   b. Camine derecho y doble a la derecha en el semáforo.

   c. Pase por el túnel y doble a la izquierda.

2. Someone asks you where the cathedral is. You need to tell them to take an exit at the traffic light.

   a. Doble a la derecha en la primera.

   b. Siga derecho hasta el semáforo.

   c. Tome la salida en el semáforo.

3. Someone asks you where the library is. You need to tell them to go along the avenue and take the second left.

   a. Siga por la avenida y doble a la izquierda en la segunda.

   b. Pase la avenida y siga derecho.

   c. Siga por esta calle y pase por el túnel.

3. Reading comprehension of cultural themes

Songs are an excellent way to learn a language. *Los caminos de la vida* (The Paths of Life) was written by Colombian composer Omar Geles. It tells the story of a man who remembers thinking as a boy that life's paths would be easier.

Now that he is grown, he realizes things are tough. But he hopes to improve his mother's life, who did so much for him when he was young.

https://youtu.be/21u11ive2kM?si=h958tfwIG1_d0LVO

Los caminos de la vida	The paths of life
no son lo que yo pensaba	are not what I thought
no son lo que yo creía	are not what I thought
no son lo que imaginaba	are not what I imagined
Los caminos de la vida	The path of life
son muy difícil de andarlos	are very difficult to walk
difícil de caminarlos	difficult to walk
y no encuentro la salida	and I can't find the way out
Yo pensaba que la vida era distinta	I thought life was different when I was a little boy, I thought
cuando era chiquitito yo creía	Things were easy, like yesterday
que las cosas eran fácil como ayer	When my concerned mother went to great lengths
Que mi madre preocupada se esmeraba	to give me everything I needed
por darme todo lo que necesitaba	And today I realize that it's not so much that way
y hoy me doy cuenta de que tanto así no es.	Because I see my mother tired
Porque a mi madre la veo cansada	of working for my brother and for me
de trabajar por mi hermano	And now I want to help her
y por mí	And for her, I'll fight till the end

y ahora con ganas quisiera ayudarla y por ella la peleo hasta el fin. Por ella lucharé hasta que me muera y por ella no me quiero morir tampoco que se me muera mi vieja* pero yo sé que el destino es así.	For her, I'll fight till I die And for her, I don't want to die I don't want my old lady to die, either But I know that destiny is like that.

* **vieja** means actually **old**, but in some Latin American countries, you can call your mother **vieja** affectionately.

Let's practice

A. Read the lyrics in Spanish and their translation in English.

B. Play a line from the song, then pause and immediately sing or say it back. Echoing the song boosts your pronunciation and intonation.

C. Try to match the following Spanish words from the song with their meaning in English.

hermano	old lady
caminos	difficult
vida	mother
madre	brother

destino	things
difícil	end
chiquitito	life
cosas	paths
vieja	little boy
fin	destiny

4. Grammar concept: Diphthongs

A diphthong is a sound made by combining two specific vowels that form one syllable, as in the **oy** sound in **oil**. The Spanish alphabet has five vowels: **a, e, i, o, u**. Two of those are weak: **i** and **u**, and three are strong: **a, e,** and **o**. In Spanish, diphthongs are formed by combining two successive weak vowels (**i, u**) or a strong vowel (**a, e,** or **o**) and a weak vowel (**i** or **u**). The important thing to remember is that both vowels form one sound. Examples of diphthongs are **bue**n, **sue**rte, Pasc**ua**, n**ue**vo, t**ie**mpo, and v**ia**jar (traveling).

When Spanish-speaking people combine words to form phrases and sentences, they pronounce them by linking them in a way that makes it almost impossible to hear the word boundaries! You can eventually understand the words and what people say with practice and patience.

Spanish Diphthongs

Diphthong	Example	English sound equivalent
ai	**ai**re (air)	eye
ay	Urugu**ay**	eye
ei ey	v**ei**nte l**ey**	hay
oi oy	pr**ohi**bido (forbidden) h**oy**	boy
ui uy	L**ui**s m**uy**	none
ia	grac**ia**s	none
ie	b**ie**n	yes
io	av**ió**n	kiosc
iu	c**iu**dad	beautiful
au	**au**tobús	couch
eu	**Eu**ropa	none
ua	c**ua**dra	water
ue	p**ue**nte	well
uo	monstr**uo**	quote

Pronunciation Practice

A. Before jumping in to practice Spanish diphthongs, let's review the pronunciation of single vowel sounds with the words below. Remember to make your vowels short and precise, avoiding dragging the **e** (which should sound like the **e** in **bet**) and the **o** (which should sound like the **o** in **low**). Utilize online pronunciation guides and resources specifically designed for language learners, such as websites that provide audio recordings of words pronounced by native speakers.

> *Hombre* (man) should not be pronounced as *hambre* (hunger)

> When the letter **y** (*and*) stands alone in Spanish, you pronounce it like the **i**. The same is true when it ends a word: **hay**.

pronto	todo	examen
año	mucho	saludos
alegro	está	noches
hola	tardes	mañana
Navidad	Amigo	blanca
rosa	corazón	calle
parque	barco	tren

B. Now pronounce these words with a diphthong:

Bien	Avión	Pie	estacionamiento
autobús	autopista	cuadra	vuele
izquierda	gracias	junio	veinte
suerte	aniversario	adiós	hacia

41

Pascua	Vuelo	Viajo	nuevo
nacionalidad	fiestas	buenas	bueno

C. The next step is to combine words with diphthongs and try to pronounce them as if they were one long word, pronounced without a pause. You can check online pronunciation resources to check your own pronunciation.

vuelo bueno (good flight)

viajo en junio (I travel in June)

nuevo aniversario (new anniversary)

autopista nueva (new highway)

cuadra izquierda (left block)

autobús nuevo (new bus)

suerte y gracias (good luck and thank you)

veinte cuadras (twenty blocks)

estacionamiento bueno (good parking)

5. Communication Tips

In the first chapter, we learned how to communicate with immigration officers when entering a country. In this chapter, we will practice the vocabulary learned earlier to find your way around a new city. In this case, you're leaving the Teatro Colón in Buenos Aires, and want to walk to your hotel but don't remember where it is.

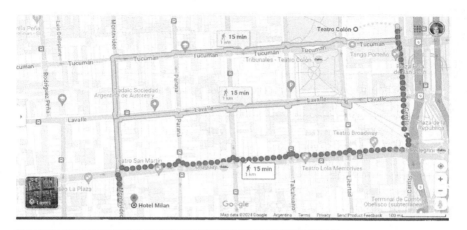

Tourist: Disculpe. ¿me puede ayudar?	Excuse me, can you help me?
Local: Por supuesto.	Of course
Tourist: Cómo llego a mi hotel?	How do I get to my hotel?
Local: ¿En qué hotel está?	What hotel are you in?
Tourist: Estoy en el hotel Milán.	I'm staying at the Milán hotel.
Local: Ah, no está lejos.	Oh, that's not far from here.
Camine hasta la calle Cerrito. Siga derecho por la calle Cerrito hacia la calle Corrientes.	Walk to Cerrito. Go straight on Cerrito Street towards Corrientes Street.
Camine dos cuadras.	Walk two blocks.
En la Avenida Corrientes, doble a la derecha.	On Corrientes Avenue, turn right.

Tourist: ¿En la Avenida Corrientes?	On Corrientes Avenue?
Local: Sí, donde está el Obelisco.	Yes, where you'll see the Obelisk.
Camine por la Avenida Corrientes	Walk on Corrientes Avenue
Pase por varios teatros, como el Teatro Broadway.	Go past several theatres, like the Broadway Theatre.
En la calle Montevideo, doble a la izquierda.	On Montevideo Street, turn to the left.
Camine media cuadra y ahí estará su hotel.	Walk half a block, and you'll find your hotel.
Tourist: Muchas gracias. Buenas noches.	Thank you very much. Good evening.
Local: Buenas noches.	Good evening.

6. Answer Key

2.

A. Doble a la izquierda: Take a left

Tome la salida 4: Take exit 4

Siga por esta calle: Go straight on this road

Tome el tren: Take the train

El teatro está a una cuadra: The theater is one block away

Cruce el paso peatonal: Cross the pedestrian crossing

Pase la biblioteca: Go past the library

La catedral está a dos cuadras The cathedral is two blocks away

Camine derecho: Walk straight on

Está a la derecha: It's on your right

Siga derecho: Go straight on

B.

a. siga	b. pase	c. doble
d. tome	e. doble	f. pase
g. doble	h. tome	i. tome

C. 1. el bar

2. el centro comercial

3. la catedral

4. la biblioteca

5. el teatro

D. 1.b

2.c

3.a

3.

C. hermano: brother

caminos: paths

vida: life

madre: mother

destino: destiny

difícil: difficult

chiquitito: little boy

cosas: things

vieja: old lady fin: end

CHAPTER 3

OUR FAMILY

1. Cultural Theme: Families in Latin America

Family ties are highly valued in Latin America. The concept of family extends beyond immediate relatives, including extended family members, such as grandparents, aunts, uncles, and cousins. They all provide emotional support and social connections. Latino people strongly think all family members have an essential role across generations, not just the working-age population. The respect for elders is an incredibly striking value: older family members are often revered for their wisdom and experience, and their contribution to the family is vital. In that sense, parents of young children have always turned to grandparents to provide childcare and help them reconcile work and family. Even when family members become physically infirm or disabled, many families believe they must provide for their parents and grandparents when they can't live by themselves, and welcome them into their homes.

2. Vocabulary

Family Members

la madre (la mamá)	mother (mom)
el padre (el papá)	father (dad)
la hija	daughter
el hijo	son
la hermana	sister
el hermano	brother
la esposa	wife
el esposo	husband
la abuela	grandmother
el abuelo	grandfather
la nieta	granddaughter
el nieto	grandson
la prima	cousin (female)
el primo	cousin (male)
la tía	aunt
el tío	uncle
la sobrina	niece
el sobrino	nephew
el suegro	father in law
la suegra	mother in law
el yerno	son in law
la nuera	daugther in law
el cuñado	brother in law
la cuñada	sister in law

You might have noticed that the words here for describing family members are preceded by **el** or **la**, the two **definite articles** in Spanish, which mean **the**. All nouns in Spanish have either masculine or feminine gender. This is only a grammatical feature of nouns and does not mean that Spanish speakers perceive things or ideas as male or female.

El defines masculine nouns while **la** describes feminine nouns (we will later see this rule is not written in stone as there are a few instances where **el** is used with feminine nouns). So **la prima** is **the cousin**, referring to a female cousin. And **el primo** is **the cousin**, referring to a male cousin. A general rule of thumb is if a word ends in **a**, it is most likely (though not always) a feminine noun, and if it ends in **o**, it is a masculine noun. So nouns like **el niño** (*the boy*) and **el amigo** (*the male friend*) just change that final vowel to express the gender: **niña** (*the girl*) and la **amiga** (*the female friend*).

Dialogue I

— Tienes una familia muy grande (you have a very large family). ¿Cuántos hermanos tienes (how many brothers do you have)?

— Tengo (I have) seis hermanos y dos hermanas.

— ¡Uf! Es un montón (it's a lot). ¿Tienes (Do you have) primos?

— Sí, tengo (I have) veinte primos.

— ¿Cuántos hermanos tiene tu madre (how many brothers does your mother have)?

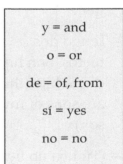

y = and

o = or

de = of, from

sí = yes

no = no

49

—Mi mamá tiene ocho hermanas y cuatro hermanos.

—¿Y cuántos hermanos tiene tu padre (how many brothers and sisters does your father have)?

—Mi padre tiene seis hermanos y una hermana.

—Ah, ¡por eso (that's why) tienes tantos primos!

Dialogue II

—¿Cuántos hijos tienes?

—Tengo una hija y dos hijos.

—¿Tienen hijos?

—Sí, tienen hijos.

—¿Cuántos nietos tienes?

—Tengo dos nietos. Son hijos de mi hijo (they are sons of my son).

—¿Tu hija no tiene hijos?

—No, mi hija no tiene hijos.

Numbers

0	cero	11	once
1	uno	12	doce
2	dos	13	trece
3	tres	14	catorce
4	cuatro	15	quince
5	cinco	16	dieciséis
6	seis	17	diecisiete
7	siete	18	dieciocho
8	ocho	19	diecinueve
9	nueve	20	veinte
10	diez		

You will see these forms of the verb **ser** (*to be*) to describe family member relationships.

(yo) **soy**	I *am*	
(tú) **eres**	you (informal) *are*	
(usted) **es**	you (formal) *are*	
(él, ella) **es**	he/she *is*	

Dialogue III

Ana and Luis are at a coffee shop and Ana is showing Luis pictures of her family vacation on her phone.

Luis: ¿Es tu familia? (Is this your family?)

Ana: Sí, es mi familia: mi papá, mi mamá, mi hermana, mi hermano y yo.

Luis: ¿Y en esta foto? (And in this picture?)

Ana: Mis abuelos y mis tíos.

Luis: ¿Son los abuelos del lado de tu madre? (Are they your grandparents on your mother's side?)

Ana: No, son los abuelos del lado de mi padre. Son Marta y Ricardo.

Luis: ¿Y tus tíos?

Ana: Es la hermana de mi padre y su esposo. Tienen dos hijos, mis primos: Sebastián y Carolina.

Luis: ¡Qué linda familia! (What a lovely family!)

Las palabras interrogativas	
¿Qué?	What?
¿Cómo?	How?
¿Cuál?	Which?
¿Cuándo?	When?
¿Cuánto?	How much? How many?
¿Dónde?	Where?
¿Quién?	Who?

Let's practice

| el abuelo Martín | la abuela María | el abuelo Juan | la abuela Rosa |

| el tío Pepe | la tía Cata | el padre Luis | la madre Paula | el tío Pedro | la tía Ana |

| el primo | la prima | la hermana | el hermano | Inés |

| José | Lila | Susy | Carlos |

> In this chapter we will see the verb **tener** a lot (*to have*). There is no need to learn the conjugation yet. It is a very irregular verb! But these forms will help you navigate the dialogues and exercises.
>
> (yo) **tengo**   I *have*
>
> (tú) **tienes**   You *have*
>
> (Nosotros) **tenemos**   We *have*
>
> (Ellos) **tienen**   They *have*

A. Complete the sentences below with the correct kinship to Inés.

Martín es el _____   Carlos es el _____   Ana es la _____

Rosa es la _____   Susy es la _____   Lila es la _____

Pepe es el _____   María es la _____   Paula es la _____

Juan es el _____   Luis es el _____   Cata es la _____

Pedro y Ana son los _____   José y Lila son los _____

Martín y María son los _____   Luis y Paula son los _____

B. Complete the sentences with the right family member according to their relationship with Inés.

Esta es la familia de Inés (This is Inés' family). Paula es la _____¹ de Luis. El tío Pedro es el ²_____ de la madre. La tía Cata es la ³_____ del padre de Inés. La abuela María es la madre del ⁴_____. La abuela Rosa es la ⁵_____ de Paula, Pedro y Ana. La tía Ana es la ₆_____ del ₇_____ Juan y de la ₈_____ Rosa. La prima Lila es la ₉_____ del primo José. El hermano Carlos es el ₁₀_____ del tío Pedro. Susy y Carlos son los ₁₁_____ de Inés. Inés es la ₁₂_____ de Luis. Pepe, Cata, Pedro y Ana son los ₁₃_____. Inés es la ₁₄_____ de la tía Cata. La prima Lila es la ₁₅_____ del tío Pepe y la tía Cata. El abuelo Juan es el ₁₆_____ de la madre, Paula. Y la abuela Rosa es la ₁₇_____ de la madre, Paula. Juan y Rosa son los ₁₈_____ de Inés. Los padres del primo José son los ₁₉_____de Inés.

C. Match the family members on the left with the English word on the right.

el abuelo	the mother
la madre	the uncle
el primo	the father
la tía	the grandparents
la abuela	the sister
el padre	the brother
los abuelos	the grandfather

la hermana	the cousin (male)
la prima	the aunt
el tío	the grandmother
el hermano	the cousin (female)

D. Answer these questions with the person's name according to the family tree.

1. ¿Quién es el esposo de la tía Cata?_____

2. ¿Quién es el hermano de Inés?_____

3. ¿Quiénes son los sobrinos de la tía Cata?_____

4. ¿Quiénes son los hermanos de la madre? _____

5. ¿Quiénes son los padres de su prima?_____

6. ¿Quiénes son los hijos de su abuela Rosa? _____

7. ¿Quiénes son los tíos de sus primos José y Lila?

   _____

8. ¿Quiénes son los abuelos de Inés?_____

9. ¿Quiénes son los nietos del abuelo Martín y la abuela María? _____

10. ¿Quiénes son los primos de su hermano Carlos?

   _____

E. ¿Quién es? Complete the following sentences.

1. El esposo de mi abuela es mi _____.

2. El hermano de mi padre es mi _____.

3. El hijo de mi tío es mi _____.

4. La madre de mi padre es mi _____.

5. La esposa de mi padre es mi _____.

3. Reading Comprehension of Cultural Theme

La familia osa

Había una vez una familia de osos que vivía en el bosque.	Once upon a time, there was a family of bears who lived in the forest
Había un papá oso, una mamá osa y un bebé oso.	There was a Father Bear, a Mother Bear, and a Baby Bear.
Un mañana, la mamá osa preparó gachas.	One morning, Mama Bear made porridge.
Mientras se enfriaba, salieron a caminar.	While it cooled, they went for a walk.
De pronto, una niña encontró la casa en el bosque.	Suddenly, a little girl found the house in the forest.
Abrió la puerta y entró.	She opened the door and entered.

Adentro, la niña vio tres platos de gachas.	Inside, the girl saw three bowls of porridge.
Primero, probó el plato del papá oso.	First, she tried Father Bear's bowl.
Luego, probó el plato de la mamá osa.	Next, she tried Mother Bear's bowl.
Finalmente, probó el plato del bebé oso.	Finally, she tried Baby Bear's bowl.
Se lo comió todo.	She ate it all.
Luego entró en la sala.	Then she went into the living room.
Había tres sillas.	There were three chairs.
La niña se sentó en la silla de papá oso.	The girl sat in Father Bear's chair.
Luego, se sentó en la silla de la mamá osa.	Next, she sat in Mother Bear's chair.
Finalmente, se sentó en la silla del bebé oso.	Finally, she sat in Baby Bear's chair.
¡Era muy cómoda!	It was so comfortable!
Después, la niña subió arriba.	Then the girl went upstairs.

Se acostó en la cama de papá oso.	She lay on Father Bear's bed.
Luego se acostó en la cama mamá osa.	Next she lay on Mother Bear's bed.
Finalmente, se acostó en la cama del bebé oso.	Finally, she lay on Baby Bear's bed.
¡Y se quedó dormida!	¡And she fell asleep!

Let's practice

A. Answer these questions about the story by choosing one of the options suggested below for each. This will help you practice the **question words** in the box a few pages earlier. Don't worry if you don't understand all the words—it's just the right difficulty level to challenge you!

una niña - una mañana - en el bosque - el plato del bebé oso - gachas - tres platos - en la cama del bebé oso - por la puerta

1. ¿Qué preparó la mamá osa? _____

2. ¿Cómo entró la niña a la casa?_____

3. ¿Qué plato se comió la niña? _____

4. ¿Cuándo preparó gachas la mamá osa? _____

5. ¿Cuántos platos de gachas había? _____

6. ¿Dónde estaba la casa de los osos? _____

7. ¿Quién entró en la casa de los osos? _____

8. ¿Dónde se quedó dormida la niña? _____

4. Grammar Concept: Nouns and Articles

You use nouns to name places, things, or ideas. In Spanish, all nouns (**los sustantivos**) have a masculine or feminine gender (**el género**). This is only a *grammatical feature* of nouns and has nothing to do with perceiving things as having male or female attributes.

Singular Masculine Nouns and Articles

Singular masculine nouns mostly end in **-o: oso.** The masculine singular noun takes the definite article **el** (*the*) or the indefinite article **un** (*a* or *an*).

el oso (*the bear*)	un hermano (*a brother*)	el abuelo (*the grandfather*)
un barco (*a boat*)	el amigo (*the friend*)	un niño (*a boy*)
el primo (*the cousin*)	un museo (*a museum*)	el plato (*the plate*)
un río (*a river*)	el sobrino (*the nephew*)	un semáforo (*a traffic light*)

∗ A common exception to this rule is the word **día,** which ends in **-a** but is masculine in gender. Other exceptions are many words that end in **-ma**: **el problema** (don't say **la problema**!).

Some masculine nouns do not end in **-o**. They either end in **-e** or in a **consonant**.

el padre (*the father*)	un hotel (*a hotel*)	el autobús (*the bus*)
un avión (*an airplane*)	el parque (*the park*)	un pasaporte (*a passport*)
el bosque (*the forest*)	un ratón (*a mouse*)	el hospital (*the hospital*)

Singular Feminine Nouns and Articles

Singular feminine nouns mostly end in **-a.** The feminine singular noun takes the definite article **la** (*the*) or the indefinite article **una** (*a or an*).

la casa (*the house*)	una tía (*an aunt*)	la hija (*the daughter*)
una vida (*a life*)	la abuela (*the grandmother*)	una niña (*a girl*)
la rosa (*the rose*)	una vieja (*an old lady*)	la familia (*the family*)
una sobrina (*a niece*)	la esposa (*the wife*)	una cama (*a bed*)

Nouns that end in **ción, -sión, -tad, -dad**, and **-tud** are also feminine: la canción (*the song*), la decisión (*the decision*), la libertad (*the freedom*), la universidad (*the university*), and la actitud (*the attitude*).

A few nouns that end in **-o** are feminine: la mano (*the hand*) and la foto (*the picture*).

Many nouns do not end in **-o** or **-a**, or even follow a pattern. Because of this, you need to learn each noun with its article:

| la clase (*the class*) | una mujer (*a woman*) | la luz (*the light*) | una flor (*a flower*) |
| la tarde (*the afternoon*) | una noche (*a night*) | el tren (*the train*) | un viaje (*a trip*) |

Nouns ending in **-ista** can be masculine or feminine, depending on whether they refer to a male or a female. How do you indicate the gender of the noun? With the article: **el/un** or **la/una**: el artista (*male artist*)/la artista (*female artist*).

The same happens with nouns ending in **-nte**: cantante (*singer*). How do you know if it's a male or female singer? From the article: **el/un** or **la/una**: el cantante (*male singer*)/la cantante (*female singer*), el estudiante (male student)/la estudiante (female student).

Some nouns that refer to persons change the **-o** masculine to the feminine ending in **-a**:

el niño (the boy)   la niña (the gir)

el amigo (the friend)   la amiga (the friend)

Other nouns that refer to a masculine person ending in a consonant add a final **-a** in the feminine:

el profesor (*the male professor*)	la profesora (*the female professor*)
el conductor (*the male driver*)	la conductora (*the female driver*)
el bailarín (*the male dancer*)	la bailarina (*the female dancer*)

Plural Masculine Nouns and Articles

The masculine plural nouns that end in a vowel add **-s** to form the plural. They take the definite article **los** (*the*) or the indefinite article **unos** (*some*).

el oso (*the bear*)	los osos (*the bears*)
un hermano (*a brother*)	unos hermanos (*some brothers*)
el abuelo (*the grandfather*)	los abuelos (*the grandfathers*)
un barco (*a boat*)	unos barcos (*some boats*)
el niño (*the boy*)	unos niños (*some boys*)

If the noun ends in -e, add an -s.

el padre (*the father*)	los padres (*the fathers*)
un bosque (*a forest*)	unos bosques (*some forests*)
el parque (*the park*)	los parques (*the parks*)

If the noun ends in a consonant, add -es.

el tren (*the train*)	los trenes (*the trains*)
un corazón (*a heart*)	unos corazones (*some hearts*)
el hotel (*the hotel*)	los hoteles (*the hotels*)
un hospital (*a hospital*)	unos hospitales (some hospitals)

If the noun ends in -z, change to -c before adding -es

un lápiz (*a pencil*)	unos lápices (*some pencils*)

Plural Feminine Nouns and Articles

The masculine plural nouns that end in a vowel add **-s** to form the plural. They take the definite article **las** (*the*) or the indefinite article **unas** (*some*).

la casa (*the house*)	las casas (*the houses*)
una hija (*a daughter*)	unas hijas (*some daughters*)
la vida (*the life*)	las vidas (*the lives*)
una abuela (*a grandmother*)	unas abuelas (some grandmothers)
la niña (*the girl*)	las niñas (*the girls*)

If the noun ends in a consonant, add **-es.**

una canción (*a song*)	unas canciones (*the songs*)
la ciudad (*the city*)	las ciudades (the cities)
una civilización (*a civilization*)	las civilizaciones (*some civilizations*)

An essential thing to remember is that in Spanish, if there are two nouns, one masculine and one feminine, and you want to group them together, you use the **masculine**. See examples below:

hermano + hermana = hermanos (*siblings*)

madre + padre = padres (*parents*)

tío + tía = tíos (*uncle and aunt*)

primo + prima = primos (*cousins*)

abuelo + abuela = abuelos (*grandparents*)

Let's practice

You might have noticed that we have been using mainly the vocabulary you've learned in these first three chapters as examples for learning nouns and articles in Spanish. The following exercises will help reinforce these words so you don't forget them!

A. Write the appropriate form of the definite article (**el/los** or **la/las**) next to each noun, depending on whether it's masculine, feminine, singular, or plural. Make sure you know the meaning of the word.

____ tarde	____noches	___ día	____ rosa	___ amigos
____ mano	___ espinas	____ cardo	___ corazones	___ pera
____ faro	____ toros	____ rana	____ ratón	___pasaportes
____ cuadra	___trenes	___autobús	____ barcos	___ taxi
____ avión	___ museos	___ restaurantes	____ hotel	___ bar

B. Write the indefinite article (**un/unos** or **una/unas**) next to each noun, depending on whether it's masculine, feminine, singular, or plural. Make sure you remember the meaning of the word.

____ biblioteca	___ parque	___ hospital	___farmacia	___teatro
____ catedral	___ banco	___ caminos	___ madre	___ tíos

____ hermanos	___ calle	___pies	____ fiesta	___autopista
___ madres	___ hija	___ abuelas	___ primo	___ nietos
____ cuñadas	___ plato	___ ríos	____ semáforo	___rosa

C. Write the plural form of the following singular nouns.
Example: la hermana <u>las hermanas</u>

el plato _____

el pie _____

la hermana _____

un lápiz _____

un abuelo _____

el corazón _____

el faro _____

el día _____

el amigo _____

una canción _____

el hotel _____

el parque _____

la ciudad _____

un niño _____

el artista _____

la noche _____

una mujer _____

la clase _____

la luz _____

una flor _____

D. Write the singular form of these plural nouns. Example:
   los niños <u>el niño</u>

los lápices _____

unas tardes _____

las noches _____

unos hospitales _____

los taxis _____

unas suegras _____

los barcos _____

unos semáforos _____

los museos _____

unos días _____

los problemas _____

unos bosques _____

unas vidas _____

las familias _____

unas camas _____

E. How would you refer to them?

El hermano y la hermana _____

El tío y la tía _____

El abuelo y la abuela _____

El primo y la prima _____

Juan y Margarita (friends) _____

Pedro y José (professors) _____

Pedro y María (professors) _____

5. Communication Tips

Learning to ask someone's name is crucial to any communication exchange. It serves as a starting point for building a personal connection, showing respect, and navigating social interactions effectively. In Spanish-speaking countries, it is considered polite to ask someone's name in any social interaction.

The use of formal (usted) and informal (tú) forms of address is based on the level of familiarity and social status between people. In each case, there are two ways to ask for someone's name.

Formal

— ¿Cómo **se** llama **usted**?	What's your name?
— Me llamo Carolina Pérez.	My name is Carolina Pérez

Informal

— ¿Cómo **te** llamas?	What's your name?
— Me llamo Carolina.	Me llamo Carolina.

Formal

— ¿Cuál[1] es **su** nombre?	What's your name?
— Mi nombre es Carolina.	My name is Carolina.

Informal

— ¿Cuál es **tu** nombre?	What's your name?
— Mi nombre es Carolina.	My name is Carolina.

6. Answer Key

2.

A.

Martín es el abuelo	Carlos es el hermano	Ana es la tía
Rosa es la abuela	Susy es la hermana	Lila es la prima

---

[1] Beginner Spanish learners might try saying «¿Qué es tu nombre?». Avoid this sentence as it sounds unusual to native speakers.

Pepe es el tío   María es la abuela   Paula es la madre

Juan es el abuelo   Luis es el padre   Cata es la tía

Pedro y Ana son los tíos   José y Lila son los primos

Martín y María son los abuelos   Luis y Paula son los padres

B.

1. esposa	11. hermanos
2. hermano	12. hija
3. hermana	13. tíos
4. padre	14. sobrina
5. madre	15. hija
6. hija	16. padre
7. abuelo	17. madre
8. abuela	18. abuelos
9. hermana	19. tíos
10. sobrino	

C.

el abuelo	the grandfather
la madre	the mother
el primo	the cousin (male)
la tía	the aunt
la abuela	the grandmother

el padre	the father
los abuelos	the grandparents
la hermana	the sister
la prima	the cousin (female)
el tío	the uncle
el hermano	the brother

D. 1. Pepe

   2. Carlos

   3. Inés, Carlos y Susy

   4. Pedro y Ana

   5. Cata y Pepe

   6. Paula, Pedro y Ana

   7. Luis, Paula, Pedro y Ana (remember **tíos** refers to both aunts and uncles)

   8. Martín, María, Juan y Rosa (remember **abuelos** refers to both grandmothers and grandfathers)

   9. José, Lila, Susy, Carlos e[2] Inés

   10. Lila y José

---

[2] Use e instead of **y** (*and*) when the next word starts with **i**

E. 1. abuelo

    2. tío

    3. primo

    4. abuela

    5. madre

3.

A.

1. gachas	5. tres platos
2. por la puerta	6. en el bosque
3. el plato del bebé oso	7. una niña
4. una mañana	8. en la cama del bebé oso

4.

A.

la tarde	las noches	el día	la rosa	los amigos
la mano	las espinas	el cardo	los corazones	la pera
el faro	los toros	la rana	el ratón	los pasaportes
la cuadra	los trenes	el autobús	los barcos	el taxi
el avión	los museos	los restaurantes	el hotel	el bar

B.

una biblioteca	un parque	un hospital	una farmacia	un teatro
una catedral	un banco	unos caminos	una madre	unos tíos
unos hermanos	una calle	unos pies	una fiesta	una autopista
unas madres	una hija	unas abuelas	un primo	unos nietos
unas cuñadas	un plato	unos ríos	un semáforo	una rosa

C.

el plato	los platos
el pie	los pies
la hermana	las hermanas
un lápiz	unos lápices
un abuelo	unos abuelos
el corazón	los corazones
el faro	los faros
el día	los días
el amigo	los amigos
una canción	unas canciones
el hotel	los hoteles
el parque	los parques
la ciudad	las ciudades

un niño	unos niños
el artista	los artistas
la noche	las noches
una mujer	unas mujeres
la clase	las clases
la luz	las luces
una flor	unas flores

D.

los lápices	el lápiz
unas tardes	una tarde
las noches	la noche
unos hospitales	un hospital
los taxis	el taxi
unas suegras	una suegra
los barcos	el barco
unos semáforos	un semáforo
los museos	el museo
unos días	un día
los problemas	el problema
unos bosques	un bosque
unas vidas	una vida
las familias	la familia
unas camas	una cama

E.

El hermano y la hermana	los hermanos
El tío y la tía	los tíos
El abuelo y la abuela	los abuelos
El primo y la prima	los primos
Juan y Margarita	los amigos
Pedro y José	los profesores
Pedro y María	los profesores

CHAPTER 4

EATING OUT

1. Cultural Theme: Meals in the Spanish-Speaking World

Eating habits in Spanish-speaking countries differ from those in other parts of the world. While it's true you can find hamburgers, steaks, and pasta everywhere, if you want an authentic cultural experience on your next trip, be prepared to try an array of unique-flavored dishes. Whether you visit Spain and indulge in their tapas (small plates of food shared among friends in bars), travel to Perú to savor their ají de gallina (creamy chicken stew), or eat an asado (a traditional meat barbecue) in Argentina, you'll gain a deeper understanding of the destination's local customs and traditions through their food. Not only do Spanish-speaking countries have their own diverse flavors, but their meal times also differ. Breakfast (**el desayuno**) is much more frugal than in the U.S., consisting mainly of coffee and milk (café con leche) and some bread; lunch (**el almuerzo**) is usually the main meal and is eaten as late as 2 p.m., and dinner (**la cena**) is lighter than lunch and usually served no earlier than 8 p.m. and even as late as 10 p.m. Because dinner is such a late affair, some people have a snack (**la merienda**) at around 5 p.m., which might consist of another café con leche and maybe a sweet roll. On your next trip, be sure to immerse yourself in the culture's rich culinary tradition!

2. Vocabulary

a. Common foods, beverages, and dishes

el pan	bread
la tostada	toast
la medialuna	croissant
el agua	water
la leche	milk
el jugo	juice
el jugo de naranja	orange juice
la gaseosa	soft drink
el café	coffee
el chocolate	chocolate
el café con leche	coffee and milk
el té	tea
el vino	wine
el vino tinto	red wine
el vino blanco	white wine
la bebida	beverage
la carne	meat
el pollo	chicken

la hamburguesa	the hamburger
el pescado	fish
el sándwich	sandwich
la ensalada	salad
la pasta	pasta
el arroz	rice
el huevo	eggs
el jamón	ham
el queso	cheese
la manzana	apple
la naranja	orange
la banana	banana
el tomate	tomato
la lechuga	lettuce
la espinaca	spinach
la zanahoria	carrot
la sopa	soup
el postre	dessert
el helado	ice cream
las verduras	vegetables

b. Restaurant-related vocabulary

el mozo (or camarero)	waiter/waitress
la cuenta	bill
el menú	menu
el pedido	order
el plato	dish
la cuchara	spoon
el tenedor	fork
el cuchillo	knife
el vaso	glass
la copa	wine glass
la servilleta	napkin
el mantel	tablecloth

c. Verbs related to eating and drinking

Tomar means many things, depending on the context!

Tomar: to drink

Tomar: to take

Comer	to eat
beber	to drink
tomar	to drink
cocinar	to cook
Preparar	to prepare

In this chapter we will see again the verb **tener** a lot (*to have*). There is no need to learn the conjugation yet. It is a very irregular verb! But these forms will help you navigate the dialogues and exercises.

(yo) **tengo**	I *have*
(tú) **tienes**	you *have*
(él/ella/usted) **tiene**	he/she has
(Nosotros) **tenemos**	we *have*
(Ellos) **tienen**	they *have*

The verb **ir** (*to go*) is another very frequent verb. Like in English, you can combine it with other verbs, like "**vamos a comer**" (*let's go eat*). It's a VERY irregular verb.

(yo) **voy**	I *go*
(tú) **vas**	you *go*
(él/ella/usted) **va**	he/she *goes*
(nosotros) **vamos**	we *go*
(ellos) **van**	they *go*

Likes and Preferences

— ¿Te gustan los aviones?

— No, no me gustan los aviones.

To indicate you like something in Spanish you say **Me gusta___**. To indicate you don't like something, you say **No me gusta_____**.

> **Vamos a** + infinitive verb= means two things:
>
> *We're going to…*
>
> *Let's go* + verb
>
> Example: **Vamos a comer** = *Let's go eat*
>
> **Vamos a comer** = *We're going to eat*

Dialogue I

Juan and Luisa are at home and feel suddenly hungry. They decide to go out to eat but don't agree on what kind of restaurant they want to go to.

Juan: Tengo hambre. ¿Comemos afuera?	I'm hungry. Shall we go out for dinner?
Luisa: Sí, yo también tengo hambre.	Yes, I'm hungry too.
¿Dónde comemos?	Where shall we eat
Juan: Vamos a comer comida china.	Let's go eat Chinese food.
¿Te gusta?	Do you like it?
Luisa: No, no me gusta la comida china.	No, I don't like Chinese food.

Juan: Entonces vamos a comer comida india.	So let's go eat Indian food.
Luisa: Tampoco me gusta la comida india.	I don't like Indian food either.
Juan: Vamos a comer pastas.	Let's go eat pasta.
Luisa: Odio las pastas.	I hate pasta
Juan: ¡No te gusta nada!	You don't like anything!
Luisa: Sí, me gustan los sandwiches.	I like sandwiches.
Juan: ¡Pero a mí no me gustan los sándwiches!	But I don't like sandwiches!

Dialogue II

Pedro and Beatriz are at a restaurant ordering food.

Pedro: ¡Disculpe, mozo! ¿Me puede traer el menú, por favor?	Excuse me, waiter! Could you please bring me the menu?
Mozo: Sí, aquí tiene.	Yes, here it is.
Beatriz: ¿Qué vas a pedir?	What are you going to order?
Pedro (to the waiter): ¿Tiene pollo con papas fritas?	Do you have chicken and French fries?

Mozo: No, no tengo papas fritas.	No, I don't have French fries.
Tengo papas al horno.	I have baked potatoes.
Pedro: Bueno, tráigame el pollo con las papas al horno, por favor.	Ok, bring me the chicken with the baked potatoes, please.
Mozo: Bueno.	Ok.
¿Y usted, señora?	And what about you, lady?
Beatriz: ¿Tiene pescado al horno?	Do you have baked fish?
Mozo: Sí, viene con una ensalada mixta de lechuga y tomate.	Yes, it's served with a mixed salad of lettuce and tomato.
Beatriz: Perfecto.	Perfect.
Pedro: ¿Me puede traer la carta de vinos, por favor?	Could you bring me the wine list, please?
Mozo: Sí, cómo no.	Yes, of course.
Beatriz: ¿Me puede traer agua, por favor?	Could you bring me water, please?
Mozo: Sí, señora.	Yes, madam.
En seguida les traigo su pedido.	I'll bring your order shortly.

Dialogue III

Beatriz and Pedro have just finished dinner and are asking for the bill.

Pedro: ¡Mozo! La cuenta, por favor.	Waiter, the bill, please.
Mozo: Aquí tiene.	Here it is.
Pedro: Gracias. ¿Cuánto es?	Thank you. How much is it?
Mozo: Son veinte dólares.	It was twenty dollars.
Pedro: ¿Puedo pagar con tarjeta de crédito	Can I pay with a credit card?
Mozo: No, solo aceptamos efectivo.	No, we only accept cash.
Pedro: Ay, no tengo efectivo.	Oh, I don't have cash.
Beatriz: Yo tengo efectivo.	I have cash.
Pedro: Gracias.	Thank you.
Beatriz (to the waiter): Tome, quédese con el vuelto.	Here, keep the change.
Mozo: Muchas gracias, señora.	Thank you very much, lady.

Let's practice

A. Here are different foods. Use **me gusta_____** and **no me gusta _____** to express which ones you like and dislike. Example: **Me gusta <u>la carne</u>.**

el pan	la leche	el jugo de naranja
el vino blanco	la gaseosa	el café	el té
el café con leche	el pollo	la carne
la hamburguesa	los sándwiches	
el pescado	la pasta	la ensalada
las verduras	el huevo	el queso
las frutas	la banana	

_____ _____ _____
_____ _____ _____
_____ _____ _____
_____ _____ _____
_____ _____ _____
_____ _____ _____
_____ _____ _____

> In Spanish, when you say *I like something*, subjects retain their articles: **el, la, los, las,** even when the English translation does without them. For example: **Me gusta el chocolate**, but *I like chocolate* (no article).

B. Pair the Spanish verbs we've seen up to now in the infinitive form (which always ends in **-r**) with **me gusta** and **no me gusta**.

Example: me **gusta <u>comer</u>** = I like eating (In English, you also pair **I like + infinitive**).

viajar (to travel)	caminar (to walk)	ir (to go)	pasar (to go by)
comer (to eat)	beber (to drink)	cocinar (to cook)	dormir (to sleep)

1. _____

2. _____

3. _____

4. _____

5. _____

6. _____

7. _____

8. _____

C. Indicate whether you like the following things or doing the following activities.

Example: ¿estudiar español? ¿estudiar alemán? ¿estudiar japonés?

<u>Me gusta estudiar español.</u>

1. ¿la música moderna? ¿la música electrónica? ¿la música clásica?

_____

2. ¿comer en casa? ¿comer en un restaurante? ¿comer en la calle?

   _____

3. ¿beber vino blanco? ¿beber vino tinto? ¿beber agua?

   _____

4. ¿viajar? ¿correr? ¿nadar (to swim)?

   _____

5. ¿los trenes? ¿los aviones? ¿el auto?

   _____

D. Say how you feel about the following people, places, or things.

   Example: la política ⟶ No me gusta la política or Me gusta la política

1. la música de Cold Play ⟶ _____
2. la comida mexicana ⟶ _____
3. los hoteles ⟶ _____
4. el dinero (money) ⟶ _____
5. el cine (the movies) ⟶ _____
6. Elon Musk ⟶ _____
7. la playa (the beach) ⟶ _____

8. Bill Gates ⟶ _____

9. la película Spider Man ⟶ _____

10. Taylor Swift ⟶ _____

3. Reading Comprehension of Cultural Theme

Here is another song called *Me gustas tú*, by Manu Chao, a French singer and activist of Spanish (Gaician-Basque) origin. He sings mainly in Spanish, French, English, and Portuguese. Quite the polyglot! The song is an upbeat track in which Chao sings about what he loves, among other things, airplanes, traveling, mornings, dreaming, the ocean, the wind, rain, mountains, and nights.

https://youtu.be/rs6Y4kZ8qtw?si=xfB4qEcTEEfLFqjC

¿Qué horas son, mi corazón?	What time is it, my love?
Te lo dije bien clarito	I said it very clearly
Permanece en la escucha	Stay listening
Permanece en la escucha	Stay listening
Doce de la noche en La Habana, Cuba	Midnight in La Habana, Cuba
Once de la noche en San Salvador, El Salvador	Eleven o'clock in the evening in San Salvador, El Salvador

86

Me gustan los aviones, me gustas tú	I like airplanes, I like you
Me gusta viajar, me gustas tú	I like traveling, I like you
Me gusta la mañana, me gustas tú	I like the morning, I like you
Me gusta el viento, me gustas tú	I like wind, I like you
Me gusta soñar, me gustas tú	I like dreaming, I like you
Me gusta la[3] mar, me gustas tú	I like the sea, I like you
¿Qué voy a hacer? Je ne sais pas	What will I do? Je ne sais pas
¿Qué voy a hacer? Je ne sais plus	What will I do? Je ne sais plus
¿Qué voy a hacer? Je suis perdu	What will I do? Je suis perdu
¿Qué horas son, mi corazón?	What time is it, my love?
Me gusta la moto, me gustas tú	I like motorcycles, I like you
Me gusta correr, me gustas tú	I like running, I like you
Me gusta la lluvia, me gustas tú	I like rain, I like you

---

[3] While the most common form is **el mar** (*the sea*), **la mar** is also grammatically correct and mostly used in poetry and songs. The plural is mostly masculine: **los mares**.

Me gusta volver, me gustas tú	I like coming back, I like you
Me gusta marihuana, me gustas tú	I like marihuana, I like you
Me gusta Colombiana, me gustas tú	I like Colombiana (may be a soft drink in Colombia), I like you
Me gusta la montaña, me gustas tú	I like mountains, I like you
Me gusta la noche (me gustas tú)	I like nighttime (I like you)
¿Qué voy a hacer? Je ne sais pas	What will I do? Je ne sais pas
¿Qué voy a hacer? Je ne sais plus	What will I do? Je ne sais plus
¿Qué voy a hacer? Je suis perdu	What will I do? Je suis perdu
¿Qué horas son, mi corazón?	What time is it, my love?
Doce, un minuto	Midnight, one minute
Me gusta la cena, me gustas tú	I like dinner, I like you
Me gusta la vecina, me gustas tú (Radio Reloj)	I like the neighbor, I like you (Radio Reloj)
Me gusta su cocina, me gustas tú (una de la mañana)	I like her cooking, I like you (one o'clock)

Me gusta camelar[4], me gustas tú	I like flirting, I like you
Me gusta la guitarra, me gustas tú	I like guitars, I like you
¿Qué voy a hacer? Je ne sais pas	What will I do? Je ne sais pas
¿Qué voy a hacer? Je ne sais plus	What will I do? Je ne sais plus
¿Qué voy a hacer? Je suis perdu	What will I do? Je suis perdu
¿Qué horas son, mi corazón?	What time is it, my love?

Let's practice

A. Answer these questions by using the information in the song to say if the author likes something or not (**le gusta** o **no le gusta**). Notice we are using the pronoun **le** because we are referring to a third person (**me** is for the person doing the talking). For example: **¿Le gusta el café (does he like coffee)? No, no le gusta el café (No, he doesn't like coffee)** (because it's not in the song).

¿Le gusta el viento (does he like the wind)? Sí, le gusta el viento (yes, he likes the wind).

---

[4] **Camelar** is a slang word, used basically in Colombia.

Also notice that when the thing liked is singular, the verb is **gusta** (third person singular), and when the thing liked is plural, the verb is **gustan** (third person plural).

1. ¿Le gustan los autos? (does he like cars)

   _____

2. ¿Le gusta soñar?

   _____

3. ¿Le gusta la bicicleta?

   _____

4. ¿Le gusta correr?

   _____

5. ¿Le gusta saltar (jumping)?

   _____

6. ¿Le gusta la nieve? (snow)

   _____

7. ¿Le gusta la montaña?

   _____

8. ¿Le gusta el piano?

   _____

9. ¿Le gusta la guitarra?

   _____

10. ¿Le gusta la cena?

    _____

B. The song has a few verbs in infinitives (verbs in Spanish belong to three groups: those whose infinitive ends in **-ar**, those that end in **-er**, and those that end in **-ir**. For example: amar, cocinar, and dormir). Try to recognize them and write them in the list with their translation.

VERB	TRANSLATION

C. After listening to the song twice, write the correct articles (feminine, masculine, singular or plural) for the nouns in the lyrics.

_____ corazón   ____ noche

_____ aviones   _____ mañana

_____ viento   _____ mar

_____ moto   _____ lluvia

_____ montaña   ____ guitarra

_____ minuto   _____ cena

4. Grammar Concept: Adjectives

Adjectives are words that describe the qualities or states of being of nouns. A Spanish adjective agrees in gender and number with the noun it modifies. For example: **perros negros** (*black dogs*). In this example, both words are masculine and plural.

91

In Spanish, most adjectives are placed **behind** the noun they describe: **desayuno abundante** (abundant breakfast).

Singular Masculine Adjectives

Singular Masculine Adjectives that end in **-o** are masculine in form and agree with the masculine noun.

el pan blanco	white bread
el pescado delicioso	delicious fish
el huevo duro	hard-boiled egg
el mozo simpático	nice waiter
el vaso limpio	clean glass
el helado frío	cold ice cream

Singular Feminine Adjectives

Adjectives that end in **-o** change to **-a** when describing a feminine noun.

la servilleta **blanca**	white napkin
la leche **deliciosa**	delicious milk
La zanahoria **dura**	hard carrot
la moza **simpática**	nice waitress
la cuchara **limpia**	clean spoon
la sopa **fría**	cold soup

Some adjectives don't end in **-o** or **-a** and have the **same form** for describing masculine and feminine nouns.

el libro **difícil**	difficult book
la novela **difícil**	difficult novel
el examen **fácil**	easy exam
la clase **fácil**	easy class
el brócoli **verde**	green broccoli
la lechuga **verde**	green lettuce

More adjectives

Some Spanish and English adjectives are cognates. This means they sound almost the same in both languages. You won't have any trouble figuring out what they mean!

a. These Spanish-English adjective cognates don't change form. They have the same ending for masculine or feminine nouns.

Cruel	Inteligente	Interesante	realista
elegante	independiente	terrible	paciente
importante	rebelde	valiente	responsable
natural	superior	normal	excelente

These Spanish-English adjective cognates change the form, ending in **-o** when they describe a masculine noun and in **-a** when next to a feminine noun.

generoso/a	religioso/a	serio/a	tímido/a	sincero/a
impulsivo/a	romántico/a	gracioso/a	delicioso/a	sabroso/a
venenoso/a	maduro/a	mediano/a	oscuro/a	crudo/a

Plural Adjectives

Adjectives that end in a vowel add **-s** to form the plural.

Singular	Plural
Blanco	blancos
delicioso	deliciosos
dura	duras
limpia	limpias
verde	verdes
importante	importantes

Adjectives that end in a consonant add **-es** to form the plural.

Singular	Plural
Fácil	faciles
difícil	difíciles
natural	naturales
normal	normales
marrón	marrones
joven	jóvenes

Colors (Los colores)

Amarillo	Yellow
rojo	red
azul	blue
verde	green
blanco	white
negro	black
anaranjado	orange
violeta	purple
gris	gray
marrón	brown

Here are some more adjectives and their opposites.

Bueno	Good	⟸⟹	Malo	Bad
Feliz	happy	⟸⟹	Infeliz	unhappy
barato	cheap	⟸⟹	Caro	expensive
gordo	fat	⟸⟹	Flaco	thin
fuerte	strong	⟸⟹	Débil	weak
grande	big	⟸⟹	Pequeño	small
viejo	old	⟸⟹	Joven	young
rico	rich	⟸⟹	Pobre	poor
corto	short	⟸⟹	Largo	long

Let's practice

A. 1. Choose one of the adjectives below and complete the sentences making the adjective **agree with the noun it's modifying**. Example: la manzana **deliciosa**.

natural   barato   delicioso   crudo
    larga difícil   pequeño   grande
   verde   rojo joven   blanco   limpio
              duro   venenoso

1. El pan _____

2. Los manteles _____

3. El examen_____

4. Las manzanas _____

5. El vino _____

6. El jugo de naranja _____

7. Los restaurantes _____

8. La ensalada _____

9. La planta (*the plant*)_____

10. El vaso _____

11. Los sándwiches _____

12. La carne _____

13. El mozo _____.

14. La zanahoria _____

15. La leche _____

B. Write the plural form for each of these phrases, making sure you change both the noun and the adjective. Example: **la lechuga verde ——→las lechugas verdes.**

1. El tren rápido _____

2. La naranja deliciosa _____

3. El restaurante grande _____

4. El libro difícil _____

5. El niño débil _____

6. El señor joven _____

7. El viento terrible _____

8. El agua natural _____

9. El mantel gris _____

10. La banana marrón _____

C. Write the opposite of these adjectives, following the example: **Roberto es pobre. ¿Y Juan? Juan es rico** (Roberto is poor. And Juan? Juan is rich).

1. La mujer es joven. ¿Y el hombre?

   _____

2. El niño es feliz. ¿Y la niña?

   _____

3. Las manzanas son baratas. ¿Y las bananas?

   _____

4. La señora es rica. ¿Y el señor?

   _____

5. El museo es pequeño. ¿Y la catedral?

   _____

6. El pescado es bueno. ¿Y la carne?

   _____

7. El padre es gordo. ¿Y el hijo?

   _____

8. El hermano es fuerte. ¿Y la hermana?

   _____

D. Guess what is being described. Answer with the verb **ser** (ser) in the third person singular: **es**. Example: **Es una fruta. Es anaranjada. Es dulce. <u>Es la naranja.</u>**

   1. Es un vegetal. Es verde. Se come en ensaladas.

   _____

   2. Es una fruta. Es amarilla. Es deliciosa.

   _____

   3. Es un animal. Vive en el mar. Se come.

   _____

   4. Es una bebida. Se bebe al desayuno. Es blanca.

   _____

   5. Es un vegetal. Es dura. Es anaranjada.

   _____

   6. Es amarillo. Es delicioso. Se come en sándwiches.

   _____

7. Es marrón. Se bebe en el desayuno. Es caliente (*hot*)

   _____

8. Es un vegetal. Es rojo. Se come en ensaladas.

   _____

9. Es un líquido. Se bebe. Es transparente.

   _____

10. Es una bebida. Tiene gas. _____

E. Match the colors to the right object. Be sure to make the adjectives agree with gender and number. Example: **lechuga: <u>verde</u>**

    amarillo   rojo   azul blanco anaranjado gris
                   marrón   negro

1. la naranja_____

2. el día _____

3. el vino _____

4. la banana _____

5. la noche _____

6. el cielo _____

7. el tomate _____

8. el café _____

5. Communication Tips

Potato omelet (tortilla de papas) is a traditional Spanish classic that has existed since 1767. As you can imagine, the recipe has changed over time, but this one is as classic as it comes.

Tortilla de papas

Ingredientes

papas	potatoes	1 kg (5 papas grandes)
huevos	eggs	5
cebolla	onion	1
aceite de oliva	olive oil	para freír
sal	salt	a gusto

Modo de preparación

Pelar las papas.	Peel the potatoes.
Picar la cebolla.	Chop the onion.
Freír la cebolla en una sartén con aceite de oliva.	Fry the onion in a skillet with olive oil.
Pelar las papas en láminas delgadas.	Peel the potatoes in thin slices.

Añadir a la sartén para cocinarlas.	Add to the frying pan to cook.
Las papas deben estar cocinadas pero no doradas.	Potatoes should be cooked but not browned.
Cuando las cebollas y las papas están listas, retirarlas.	When onions and potatoes are cooked, set them apart.
Batir los huevos con la sal.	Beat the eggs with the salt.
Añadir las papas y las cebollas.	Add the potatoes and onions.
Calentar un poco de aceite de oliva en una sartén.	Heat some olive oil in a skillet.
Verter la mezcla de papas en la sartén.	Pour the potato mixture in the skillet.
Cocinar a fuego medio.	Cook at medium heat.
Voltear la tortilla con un plato.	Turn the tortilla over with a plate.
Cocinar por ambos lados hasta que esté dorada.	Cook on both sides until golden brown.
Servir y disfrutar!	Serve and enjoy!

6. Answer Key

2.

A. Answers may vary.

B. Answers may vary.

C. Answers may vary.

D. Answers may vary.

3.

A. 1. No, no le gustan los autos.

2. Sí, le gusta soñar.

3. No, no le gustan las bicicletas.

4. Sí, le gusta correr.

5. No, no le gusta saltar.

6. No, no le gusta la nieve

7. Sí, le gusta la montaña.

8. No, no le gusta el piano.

9. Sí, le gusta la guitarra.

10. Sí, le gusta la cena.

B.

VERB	TRANSLATION
viajar	to travel
soñar	to dream
hacer	to do
correr	to run
volver	to come back

C.

el corazón	la noche	los aviones	la mañana
el viento	la mar	la moto	la lluvia
la montaña	la guitarra	el minuto	la cena

4.

A. 1. El pan duro

2. Los manteles limpios

3. El examen difícil

4. Las manzanas rojas

5. El vino blanco

6. El jugo de naranja natural

7. Los restaurantes baratos

8. La ensalada verde

9. La planta venenosa

10. El vaso pequeño

11. Los sándwiches grandes

12. La carne cruda

13. El mozo joven

14. La zanahoria larga

15. La leche deliciosa

B.

1. Los trenes rápidos

2. Las naranjas deliciosas.

3. Los restaurantes grandes.

4. Los libros difíciles.

5. Los niños débiles.

6. Los señores jóvenes.

7. Los vientos terribles.

8. Las aguas naturales.

9. Los manteles grises.

10. Las bananas marrones.

C.

1. El hombre es viejo.

2. La niña es infeliz

3. Las bananas son caras.

4. El señor es pobre.

5. La catedral es grande.

6. La carne es mala.

7. El hijo es delgado.

8. La hermana es débil.

D.

1. Es la lechuga.

2. Es la banana.

3. Es pescado.

4. Es leche.

5. Es la zanahoria.

6. Es queso.

7. Es café.

8 Es tomate.

9. Es agua.

10. Es una gaseosa.

E.

1. la naranja: anaranjada

2. el día: gris

3. el vino: blanco

4. la banana: amarilla

5. la noche negra

6. el cielo azul

7. el tomate rojo

8. el café marrón

CHAPTER 5

LET'S GO SHOPPING

1. Cultural Theme: Shopping in Spanish-speaking countries

Due to cultural differences and consumer behavior, shopping can vary significantly between the United States and Spanish-speaking countries. While shopping malls have been popular in Latin America and Spain for decades, people generally prefer shopping at smaller neighborhood stores and markets. These local stores have a more limited selection of items but are conveniently located next to people's homes. Whether it's a fruit and vegetable store, the butcher's, the deli, or the bakery, they specialize in fresh, often locally sourced goods. Frequent visits allow for personal interactions and building trust between customers and owners, creating a strong sense of community. Another critical difference is that shopping is often seen as a leisure activity in the United States. People spend many hours browsing stores, comparing prices, and looking for deals and discounts. In Latin America, shopping is more task-oriented: people go to stores to buy a specific item, focusing on things they need, and rarely feel tempted to buy something that wasn't in their plans.

2. Vocabulary

a. Clothes stores

el pantalón	pants
el jean	blue jeans
el short	shorts
el vestido	dress
la falda	skirt
la camisa	shirt
la corbata	tie
la blusa	blouse
la camiseta	T-shirt
el suéter	sweater
el buzo (sudadera in Spain)	sweatshirt
el abrigo	coat
la chaqueta	jacket
el traje	suit
el pijama	pajama
el impermeable	raincoat
el paraguas	umbrella
el traje de baño	bathing suit
el sombrero	hat
el cinturón	belt
las medias (calcetines in Spain)	socks
un par de medias	a pair of socks

los zapatos	shoes
el par de zapatos	pair of shoes
los tacos	highheels
las zapatillas/zapatillas deportivas	sneakers
las botas	boots
un par de botas	a pair of boots
las sandalias	sandals
las pantuflas	slippers
la cartera	purse in Latin America/wallet in Spain
la bolsa	purse in Spain/bag in Latin America
el reloj	watch
las flores	flowers
lana	wool
cotton	algodón
seda	silk
probador	changing room
grande	big
mediano	medium
small	small
justo	tight
manga	sleeve
manga corta	short sleeve
manga larga	long sleeve

b. Food stores

la panadería	bakery
la pescadería	fish store
la carnicería	butcher
la frutería y verdulería	fruits and vegetables store
la fiambrería	deli
la farmacia	drugstore
el supermercado	supermarket
la ferretería	hardware store
el bar	the bar
el centro	downtown
el centro comercial	shopping mall
la tienda departamental	department store
la tienda	store
la zapatería	shoe store
la florería	flower store
el mercado	market
el precio	price
barato	cheap
caro	expensive

c. Verbs related to shopping

Comprar	to buy
vender	to sell

enseñar	to show
regatear	to bargain, to haggle
llevar	to wear, to carry, to take
vestirse	to dress
necesitar	to need
probar	to try on
usar	to wear
quedar	to fit

Let's practice

A. It's time to practice some numbers! Solve these problems by reading them aloud. Follow the models:

15 + 3 = 18 quince **más** tres **es igual a** dieciocho (fifteen plus three equals eighteen).

20 - 9 = 11 veinte **menos** nueve **es igual a** once (twenty minus nine equals eleven).

1. 1 + 4 =	4. 1 - 1 + 3 =	7. 8 + 7 =	10. 13 - 9 =
2. 3 + 5 + 6 =	5. 4 + 4 =	8. 6 - 2 =	11. 10 + 1 =
3. 30 - 20 =	6. 18 - 6 =	9. 20 - 17 =	12. 24 + 3 =

B. Using an online pronunciation guide to compare your pronunciation to native speakers, practice saying these numbers aloud.

1. 6 niños	6. 1 manzana (fem)	11. 28 pantalones
2. 13 tenedores	7. 21 minutos (masc)	12. 5 noches

3. 1 té (masc)	8. 15 mañanas	13. 20 autos
4. 21 cafés (masc)	9. 8 zanahorias	14. 30 camisas
5. 4 hamburguesas	10. 1 sombrero (masc)	15. 7 cinturones

C. Check out the box above explaining the verb **hay** (*there is* and *there are*) from the verb **haber**. Answer these questions using **hay** + number in words. Example: **¿Cuántas hamburguesas hay en el plato?** (*How many hamburgers are there on the plate?* **Hay dos hamburguesas en el plato** (*There are two hamburgers on the plate*).

1. ¿Cuántos pares de zapatos hay en el clóset? (5)

   _____

2. ¿Cuántos tenedores hay en la mesa?(10)

   _____

3. ¿Cuántos paraguas hay en la casa (house)? (9)

   _____

4. ¿Cuántas bananas hay en la frutera (fruit bowl)? (1)

   _____

5. ¿Cuántas carnicerías hay en tu ciudad (your city)? (17)

   _____

6. ¿Cuántos centros comerciales hay en tu barrio (neighborhood)? (1)

   _____

7. ¿Cuántos vestidos hay en el clóset de María? (12)

   _____

8. ¿Cuántas aspirinas hay en la farmacia? (30)

_____

9. ¿Cuántos relojes hay en la casa? (4)

_____

10. ¿Cuántos pijamas hay en el cajón (drawer)? (13)

_____

D. We have already studied **un** and **una** in Chapter 3, but we will practice them now with the new vocabulary relating to clothes. Write the masculine singular indefinite article **un** (*a*) or the feminine singular indefinite article **una** (*a*) or their plural forms, **unos** or **unas**, before each noun, depending on their gender.

1. ___ vestido	6. ___ pantalón	11. ___ jean
2. ___ falda	7. ___ camisa	12. ___ suéter
3. ___ pijama	8. ___ abrigo	13. ___ par de medias
4. ___ zapatillas	9. ___ sandalias	14. ___ corbata
5. ___ pantuflas	10. ___ reloj	15. ___ flores

Dialogue I

Clara is browsing through clothes in a store.

Vendedor: ¿Puedo ayudarla?	Salesperson: Can I help you?
Clara: Gracias. Estoy mirando.	Clara: Thanks. I'm browsing.
Vendedor: Tómese su tiempo.	Salesperson: Take your time.

Clara: Muchas gracias.	Clara: Thanks a lot.
Vendedor: Si necesita ayuda, pídala.	Salesperson: If you need help, ask for it.
Clara: Gracias. Muy amable.	Clara: Thanks. That's very kind of you.

Dialogue II

Elena is in a store looking for a dress.

Elena: Buenas tardes.	Elena: Good afternoon.
Vendedor: ¿Puedo ayudarla?	Salesperson: Can I help you?
Elena: ¿Puede enseñarme vestidos?	Elena: Can you show me some dresses?
Vendedor: Sí, cómo no.	Salesperson: Yes, of course.
Elena: ¿Puedo probarme este vestido?	Elena: Can I try this dress on?
Vendedor: Sí, claro.	Salesperson: Of course.
Elena: ¿Lo tiene en azul?	Elena: Do you have it in blue?
Vendedor: Sí, aquí tiene.	Salesperson: Yes, here it is.
¿Qué talla lleva?	What size do you wear?

Elena: Llevo un talle pequeño.	Elena: I wear a size small.
¿Puedo probármelo?	Can I try it on?
Vendedor: Por supuesto.	Salesperson: Of course.
Elena: ¿Dónde está el probador?	Elena: Where is the changing room?
vendedor: Está allá.	Salesperson: It's right over there.
Elena: Gracias.	Elena: Thank you.
vendedor: De nada.	Salesperson: You're welcome.

Dialogue III

Elena has tried the dress on, but it's too small.

Vendedor: ¿Cómo le quedó el vestido?	Salesperson: How did the dress fit you?
Elena: Me queda demasiado justo.	Elena: It's too tight.
¿Tiene una talla más grande?	Do you have a larger size?
Vendedor: Sí. Aquí tiene.	Salesperson: Yes, here it is.
Elena: Gracias.	Elena: Thank you.

Vendedor: ¿Y este cómo le queda?	Salesperson: And how does this one fit you?
Elena: Me queda bien.	Elena: It fits me well.
vendedor: ¿Lo lleva?	Salesperson: Will you take it?
Elena: Sí, lo llevo.	Elena: Yes, I'll take it.
vendedor: Adiós.	Salesperson: Good bye.
Elena: Hasta pronto.	Elena: See you soon.

E. Match the items on the left with the store where you can find them on the right.

las botas	la pescadería
el vestido	la florería
el café con leche	la farmacia
el pescado	la fiambrería
la carne	la zapatería
el pan	la tienda departamental
la falda	la carnicería
las aspirinas	el bar
el reloj	la panadería
el jamón	el centro comercial
las flores	la relojería

F. Place the following clothing items in the right season: **el verano** (summer) or **el invierno** (winter).

el vestido de lana	el traje de baño	las botas
el vestido de algodón	el short	el suéter
la blusa de manga larga	las sandalias	las medias
la blusa de manga corta	el abrigo	la camiseta

VERANO	INVIERNO

G. It's your turn to do a closet inventory!

Think about the following garments you own and write the number of pieces you have in your closet. Use the verb **tener** (*to have* or *to own*). Example: **Tengo cuatro jeans** (*I own four jeans*).

vestidos - pantalones - jeans - shorts - camisas - corbatas - camisetas - suéteres - buzos - abrigos - chaquetas - trajes de baño - cinturones - zapatos - botas - relojes

_____

_____

_____

_____

_____

_____

H. In Chapter 4, we learned colors. Choose a color and a clothing item to express what you like. Be sure to write **gustan** as you will be referring to items in general. And remember to match the adjective to the noun's gender and number. Example: **Me gustan los pantalones negros** (not **Me gusta los pantalones negro**) or **Me gustan las blusas blancas.**

<u>Colores</u>: amarillo - azul - rojo - anaranjado - verde - negro - blanco - marrón

<u>Prendas de ropa</u>: vestidos - zapatillas - abrigos - corbatas- chaquetas - pantalones - suéteres - trajes

1. _____

2. _____

3. _____

4. _____

5. _____

6. _____

7. _____

8. _____

¿Qué ropa llevan? Translate the clothing items and their articles (**un/unos** or **una/unas**) to describe what each person is wearing.

Example: **El Sr. Pérez lleva <u>un abrigo</u>, <u>un sombrero</u> y <u>unas medias.</u>**

(a coat)   (a hat)   (socks)

1. La Sra. Zorrilla lleva _____, _____ y _____.

(a dress)   (a sweater)   (high heels)

2. Miguel lleva _____, _____ y _____.

(a suit)   (a shirt)   (a tie)

3. Pedro lleva _____, _____ y _____.

(a short)   (a T-shirt)   (sneakers)

4. María lleva _____ y _____.

(a bathing suit)   (a hat)

5. Luisa lleva _____, _____ y _____

(pants)   (a blouse)   (pair of boots)

6. Sebastián lleva _____, _____ y _____.

(a suit)   (a raincoat)   (a hat)

7. Teresa lleva _____, _____ y _____.

(a skirt)   (a shirt)   (sandals)

8. José lleva _____, _____ y _____.

(pants)   (a shirt)   (a coat)

9. Marcos lleva _____, _____ y _____.

(a pajama)   (socks)   (slippers)

10. Margarita lleva _____ y _____.

(a dress)   (high heels)

3. Reading Comprehension of Cultural Theme

This is a poem called **Llega el invierno** (Winter is here) by Spanish children's author Marisol Perales, and it tells about the quest of winter in search of the sun.

El señor invierno	Mr. Winter
se viste de blanco	dresses in white
se pone el abrigo	he puts his coat on
porque está temblando.	because he's shivering.
Se va a la montaña	He goes to the mountains
se mete en el río	he gets into the river
y el parque y la calle	and the park and the street
se llenan de frío.	are filled up with cold.
Se encuentra a la lluvia	He finds the rain
llorando, llorando	crying, crying
y también al viento	and also the wind
que viene soplando.	that comes blowing.
¡Ven, amigo sol!	Come, my sunny friend!
grita en el camino,	he shouts on the road,
pero el sol no viene	but the sun doesn't come
porque se ha dormido.	because it has fallen asleep.

Let's practice

A. Match the questions with the correct answers. These exercises help you practice question words or interrogative pronouns, like **qué, cómo, por qué, dónde**.

1. ¿Qué se pone el señor   Llorando
   Invierno?

2. ¿Cómo está la lluvia?   Porque se ha dormido

3. ¿Por qué el Sr. Invierno se Se pone un abrigo
   pone el abrigo?

4. ¿Dónde se mete el Sr.   Porque está temblando
   Invierno?

5. ¿Cómo viene el viento?   En el río

6. ¿Por qué no viene el Sol?   Viene soplando

B. Fill in the crossword puzzle with the word in Spanish.

ACROSS	DOWN
3. park	1. street
4. mountain	2. white
8. river	5. coat
9. wind	6. cold
	7. sun

4. Grammar Concept: Stress and Written Accent Marks in Spanish

In the words **helado, mamá,** and *número*, as well as in all words in Spanish, there is one particular syllable that is stressed or given more emphasis than the others, whether it has an accent mark or not. In Spanish, the stress in words can be predicted based on the word's written form.

a. If a word ends in n, s, or a vowel, the stress falls typically on the next-to-the-last syllable.

   ca**mi**no - le**chu**ga - e**xa**men - ves**ti**do - a**bri**go - **po**llo

b. If the word ends in any other consonant, the stress falls typically on the last syllable.

   se**ñal** - proba**dor** - cate**dral** - hospi**tal** - ciu**dad** - Navi**dad**

c. Any exception to these two rules will have a written accent mark on the stressed vowel.

   a**vión** - **tú**nel - per**dón** - ma**má** - me**nú** - ca**fé** - cora**zón**

d. Accent marks may vary when words switch from singular to plural to keep the original stress pattern when words are made plural.

examen	exámenes
joven	jóvenes
nación	naciones

e. When one-syllable words have a written accent, the reason is to distinguish them from the exact version of the word that means something else. For example:

té (*tea*) vs. **te** (*you*)

sí (*yes*) vs. **si** (*if*)

él (*he*) vs. **el** (*the*)

tú (*you*) vs. **tu** (*your*)

f. Interrogative and exclamatory words also have a written accent on the stressed syllable. For example: **¿Quién es?** (*Who is it?*), **¿Qué come?** (*What is he eating?*), **¿Dónde va?** (*Where is he/she going?*).

Let's practice

A. Practice pronouncing these words, making sure to stress the correct vowel. You can compare your pronunciation to any recorded version of the Spanish sounds on the Internet.

1.

hijo	madre	padre	viejo	grande
hermana	sobrina	sincero	crudo	oscuro
pequeño	verdes	blanco	negro	joven

2.

pagar	azul	picar	disfrutar	cocinar
calentar	comprar	mujer	general	batir

3.

sartén	difícil	débil	marrón	fácil
romántico	música	cómo	lápiz	ratón

B. Indicate the stressed vowel of each word and give the rule that determines the stress of each word (a, b, or c).

1. lápiz _____

2. hombre _____

3. vende _____

4. natural _____

5. corazón _____

6. jugo _____

7. mantel _____

8. menú _____

9. música _____

10. simpático _____

C. True or false? Circle the correct answer.

1. A word ending in -n, -s, or a vowel is usually stressed on the last syllable.

        True   False

2. A word ending in any other consonant is typically stressed on the next-to-last-syllable

        True   False

3. Any exception to these two rules requires a written accent on the stressed consonant.

        True   False

4. A word ending in -n, -s, or a vowel is usually stressed on the next-to-last-syllable

        True   False

5. A word ending in any other consonant is typically stressed on the last syllable.

        True   False

6. Any exception to these two rules requires a written accent on the stressed vowel.

True   False

5. Communication Tips

Haggling, or bargaining, is a standard part of the shopping experience in many Latin American countries, especially in markets, street stalls, and smaller shops. In fact, vendors expect some level of negotiation. Negotiating in Spanish is obviously advantageous, as it demonstrates your familiarity with the culture and may help you establish a stronger rapport with the vendor. So sharpen your skills and prepare to go out in the streets on your next trip to a Spanish-speaking country!

Compradora: ¡Buenas tardes!	Buyer: Good afternoon!
Vendedor: ¡Buenas tardes! ¿Busca algo en especial?	Seller: Good afternoon! Are you looking for anything special?
Compradora: Me gusta este pañuelo. ¿Cuánto cuesta?	Buyer: I like this scarf. How much is it?
Vendedor: Cuesta cien pesos.	Seller: It costs one hundred pesos.
Compradora: Ay, es muy caro. ¿Me lo deja en cincuenta pesos?	Buyer: Oh, that's too expensive. Can I have it for eighty pesos?
Vendedor: Ay, no puedo, señora. Es de seda.	Seller: Oh, I can't, lady. It's silk.

125

Comprador: ¡Qué lástima! Adiós.	Buyer: What a shame. Goodbye.
Vendedor: ¡Espere! Puedo bajarlo a ochenta pesos.	Seller: Wait! I can let you have it for eighty pesos.
Comprador: Si me lo deja en setenta pesos, lo llevo.	Buyer: If you let me have it for seventy pesos, I'll take it.
Vendedor: Está bien. Se lo dejo en setenta pesos.	Seller: Ok. You can have it for seventy pesos.
Comprador: ¡Muchas gracias!	Buyer: Thank you very much!
Vendedor: De nada.	Seller: You're welcome.

6. Answer Key

2.

A.

1. Uno más cuatro es igual a cinco.

2. Tres más cinco más seis es igual a catorce.

3. Treinta menos veinte es igual a diez.

4. Uno menos uno más tres es igual a tres.

5. Cuatro más cuatro es igual a ocho.

6. Dieciocho menos seis es igual a doce.

7. Ocho más siete es igual a quince.

8. Seis menos dos es igual a cuatro.

9. Veinte menos diecisiete es igual a tres.

10. Trece menos nueve es igual a cuatro.

11. Diez más uno es igual a once.

12. Veinticuatro más tres es igual a veintisiete.

C.

1. Hay cinco pares de zapatos en el clóset.

2. Hay diez tenedores en la mesa.

3. Hay nueve paraguas en la casa.

4. Hay una banana en la frutera.

5. Hay diecisiete carnicerías en mi ciudad.

6. Hay un centro comercial en mi barrio.

7. Hay doce vestidos en el clóset de María.

8. Hay treinta aspirinas en la farmacia.

9. Hay cuatro relojes en la casa.

10. Hay trece pijamas en el cajón.

D.

1. un vestido	6. un pantalón	11. un jean
2. una falda	7. una camisa	12. un suéter
3. un pijama	8. un abrigo	13. un par de medias
4. unas zapatillas	9. unas sandalias.	14. una corbata
15. unas pantuflas	10. un reloj	15. unas flores

E.

las botas	la zapatería
el vestido	el centro comercial *or* la tienda departamental
el café con leche	el bar
el pescado	la pescadería
la carne	la carnicería
el pan	la panadería
la falda	el centro comercial *or* la tienda departamental
las aspirinas	la farmacia
el reloj	la relojería
el jamón	la fiambrería
las flores	la florería

F.

VERANO	INVIERNO
el vestido de algodón	el vestido de lana
el traje de baño	la blusa de manga larga
el short	las botas
las sandalias	el suéter
la blusa de manga corta	las medias
la camiseta	el abrigo

G. Answers vary. Some could be: Tengo tres vestidos, tengo dos shorts, tengo dos abrigos, tengo tres trajes de baño, and so on.

H. Answers may vary, but here are some suggestions:

1. Me gustan los vestidos verdes.
2. Me gustan las zapatillas rojas.
3. Me gustan los abrigos negros.
4. Me gustan las corbatas azules.
5. Me gustan las chaquetas blancas.
6. Me gustan los pantalones anaranjados.
7. Me gustan los suéteres amarillos.
8. Me gustan los trajes marrones.

I.

1. La Sra. Zorrilla lleva un vestido, un suéter y unos tacos.
2. Miguel lleva un traje, una camisa y una corbata.
3. Pedro lleva un short, una camiseta y unas zapatillas.
4. María lleva un traje de baño y un sombrero.
5. Luisa lleva unos pantalones, una blusa y un par de botas.
6. Sebastián lleva un traje, un impermeable y un sombrero.

7. Teresa lleva una falda, una camisa y unas sandalias.

8. José lleva unos pantalones, una camisa y un abrigo.

9. Marcos lleva un pijama, unas medias y unas pantuflas.

10. Margarita lleva un vestido y unos tacos.

3.

A.

1. Se pone un abrigo.

2. Llorando.

3. Porque está temblando.

4. En el río.

5. Viene soplando.

6. Porque se ha dormido.

B.

ACROSS	DOWN
3. parque	1. calle
4. montaña	2. blanco
8. río	5. abrigo
9. viento	6. frío
	7. sol

4.

B.

1. la (rule c)

2. hom (rule a)

3. ven (rule a)

4. al (rule b)

5. zón (rule c)

6. ju (rule a)

7. tel (rule b)

8. nú (rule c)

9. mú (rule c)

10. pá (rule c)

C.

1. False

2. False

3. False

4. True

5. True

6. True

Make a Difference with Your Review

Unlock the Power of Generosity

"Knowledge shared is knowledge multiplied."

- Robert Noyce

Hi there, friend!

First off, thank you for choosing to spend your time with our **Spanish Workbook for Adults**. It means the world to us, and we hope you're finding it valuable and enjoyable.

Now, I have a small favor to ask...

Would you help someone you've never met, even if you never got credit for it?

This person is just like you were not too long ago. They're eager to learn Spanish, looking to improve their skills, and searching for the right resources.

Our mission at Morelingua Academy is to make learning Spanish accessible to everyone. Everything we do stems from that mission, and the only way we can accomplish it is by reaching... well, everyone.

This is where you come in. Most people do, in fact, judge a book by its cover (and its reviews). So here's my ask on behalf of a fellow language learner you've never met:

Please help that language learner by leaving this book a review.

Your gift costs no money and less than 60 seconds to make real, but can change a fellow learner's life forever. Your review could help...

...one more person achieve fluency.

...one more learner gain confidence.

...one more student find joy in learning.

...one more dream come true.

To get that 'feel good' feeling and help this person for real, all you have to do is... and it takes less than 60 seconds... leave a review.

If you feel good about helping a fellow learner, you are my kind of person. Welcome to the club. You're one of us.

I'm that much more excited to help you master Spanish faster and easier than you can possibly imagine. You'll love the tips, exercises, and insights I'm about to share in the coming chapters.

Thank you from the bottom of my heart. Now, back to our regularly scheduled programming.

- Your biggest fan,

Morelingua Academy

PS - Fun fact: If you provide something of value to another person, it makes you more valuable to them. If you believe this book will help them, send it their way.

CHAPTER 6

WHAT BIG EYES YOU HAVE

1. Cultural Theme: Reaching Out

In recent years, there has been a noticeable trend in many Western countries towards valuing personal space and maintaining physical distance in social interactions. One of the reasons may be an increased emphasis on individualism, which may contribute to a desire for personal boundaries. While it certainly is a step toward becoming more mindful of our actions and refraining from touching others without their consent, Spanish-speaking countries have a more relaxed view of physical interactions. People in Latin America and Spain value warmth, expressiveness, and emotional connection in social interactions. This manifests in more frequent hugging, kissing on the cheek, and other forms of physical affection among family and friends. Foreigners sometimes wonder about the displays of physical affection compared to other countries; football players are an example of this. So don't be surprised if someone greets you on your next trip to South America with a light-hearted peck on the cheek!

2. Vocabulary

a. Body parts

la cabeza	head
el pelo	hair
el cabello	hair
la cara	face
la frente	forehead
el cuello	neck
la oreja	ear
el ojo	eye
el párpado	eyelid
la ceja	eyebrow
la pestaña	eyelash
la nariz	nose
la boca	mouth
la lengua	tongue
el mentón	chin
la mejilla	cheek
el diente	tooth
el cuerpo	body
el pecho	chest
el torso	torso
el hombro	shoulder
el estómago	stomach

el ombligo	belly button
el pubis	pubis
el hueso	bone
la cadera	hip
la cintura	waist
la espalda	back
la pierna	leg
el muslo	thigh
la rodilla	knee
la pantorrilla	calf
el tobillo	ankle
el talón	heel
el pie	foot
el dedo gordo	toe
el brazo	arm
el codo	elbow
el antebrazo	forearm
la muñeca	wrist
la mano	hand
el dedo	finger

b. Body organs

el corazón	heart
el estómago	stomach
la garganta	throat

el riñón	kidney
el hígado	liver
el intestino	intestine
el esófago	oesophagus
el pancreas	pancreas
el pulmón	lung
la sangre	blood
los nervios	nerves
la piel	skin

c. Verbs and other health-related words

dolor	pain
paciente	patient
tirita (in Spain) and curita (in AmL)	band-aid
duele	it hurts
tener fiebre	have a fever
tiene que	you have to
tomar una aspirina	take an aspirin
tomar un remedio	take medicine
tener una infección	have an infection
tomarse la temperatura	take the temperature
ponerse una inyección	get a shot
ir al médico	go to the doctor
tomar agua	drink water

tomar un antibiótico	take an antibiotic
hacer reposo	rest
hacer una dieta especial	follow a special diet

Let's practice

A. Label the parts of the body

Label the Parts of the Body

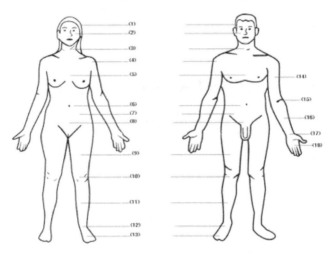

Label the Parts of the Face

B. Search for the body parts in this word search:

~~~~~~~~~ **BODY PARTS - EL CUERPO** ~~~~~~~~~

```
C D E C A S I P H G M V I G Y C P Q O
J D N L G A Q P U E K V F N O S E R N
E X F P A N C R E A S G V Z I S L R M
O C T T R R V N S C Q C P Y P D O P T
A B A V G E J Z O P H N I I N G Q L E
M Z J Y A I B Z S I E O E N A S O E D
D H E Q N P I I S R N L S M T M Z R Y
X M C B T R R G V F B T O W C U A G F
D E A F A L L I D O R T E Y C W R N G
N T X N C C O L Y I S L Z S W X B A D
T G Z I O S Q O R E J A K L T K V S C
N O G A F O S E X C N L N O T I X K R
S O D E D C Q W A K E O R W H P N N K
D A S A G J G D B P D G M G H Q O O F
U R R H P N E M Y A E K I L G P I M V
C H O M B R O F G X T N V F U W Z G N
V J H J A U A I Q K G Y Y N D P X Y U
O Z H H X D H P E U N V M D D A X O Y
```

NARIZ	INTESTINO	CABEZA	PULMON
OJO	ESOFAGO	PELO	GARGANTA
PARPADO	OREJA	CADERA	PIERNAS
CEJA	BRAZO	RODILLA	PIES
PIEL	MANO	HUESOS	PECHO
ESTOMAGO	DEDOS	SANGRE	CINTURA
HIGADO	HOMBRO	NERVIOS	PANCREAS

SPANISH WORD SEARCH BY SOFIA JAMES DE LA VEGA. WWW.SPANISHWORDSEARCH.COM - ALL RIGHTS RESERVED

C. ¿Verdadero o falso? Circle the correct answer in each case. We're practicing the verb **tener** (*to have*) again, together with the **numbers**.

1. Un cuerpo tiene tres cabezas   verdadero   falso

2. Una cara tiene dos ojos   verdadero   falso

3. Un brazo tiene una muñeca   verdadero   falso

4. La pierna entra (goes into) en el zapato   verdadero   falso

5. El pie entra (goes into) en el zapato   verdadero   falso

6. La comida entra (goes into) en la oreja   verdadero   falso

7. Un cuerpo tiene cinco brazos	verdadero	falso
8. La cabeza tiene ocho narices	verdadero	falso
9. Una mano tiene cinco dedos	verdadero	falso
10. La sangre es azul	verdadero	falso
11. El hígado está en la cabeza	verdadero	falso
12. El corazón bombea (pumps) sangre	verdadero	falso

D. Join the Spanish word on the left with its equivalent in English on the right. Try to study the words in Spanish first, so you don't need to peek!

ojo	shoulder
boca	toe
oreja	stomach
nariz	thigh
cabello	mouth
cara	elbow
cuello	waist
hombro	eye
espalda	ear
pecho	hip
estómago	knee
cintura	chest
muñeca	heel
codo	hair
rodilla	neck

tobillo	back
talón	face
dedo gordo	ankle
cadera	wrist
muslo	nose

E. What would you say to your patient if you were a doctor? Again, the verb **tener** shows up, but this time together with **que**: **tener que** means *to have to.* These are the possible options:

tomar una aspirina	tomarse la temperatura
ponerse una inyección de cortisona	ponerse una tirita
tomar agua	tomar un antibiótico
hacer reposo	hacer una dieta especial

1. El paciente tiene fiebre:

Tiene que (he has to) _____

2. El paciente tiene dolor de cabeza:

Tiene que (he has to) _____

3. El paciente está deshidratado (dehydrated).

Tiene que (he has to) _____

4. El paciente se torció el pie (sprained his foot).

Tiene que (he has to) _____

5. El paciente tiene una infección en el diente (has a tooth infection).

Tiene que (he has to) _____

6. El paciente tiene un malestar estomacal (has an upset stomach).

Tiene que (he has to) _____

7. El paciente se cortó (cut) el dedo.

Tiene que (he has to) _____

8. El paciente tiene una contractura (has a contracture).

Tiene que (he has to) _____

Dialogue I

Sometimes, healing is easier than you think! Mrs. Díaz went to the doctor about the pain she was experiencing in her arm. The doctor gave her a simple suggestion to get rid of it.

Doctor: Buenos días, señora Díaz.	Doctor: Good morning, Mrs. Díaz
Señora Díaz: Buenos días, doctor.	Señora Díaz: Good morning, doctor.
Doctor: ¿Qué le duele?	Doctor: ¿What is hurting?
Señora Díaz: Doctor, me duelen los brazos.	Señora Díaz: Doctor, my arms hurt.
Doctor: ¿Dónde le duele?	Doctor: Where does it hurt?
Señora Díaz: Me duele el codo.	Señora Díaz: My elbow hurts.

Doctor: ¿Cuál es su actividad?	Doctor: What is your activity?
Señora Díaz: Soy escritora.	Señora Díaz: I'm a writer.
Doctor: Ah, ya sé.	Doctor: Oh, I know.
Señora Díaz: ¿Qué?	Señora Díaz: What?
Doctor: El dolor es por la posición de los brazos cuando trabaja en la computadora.	Doctor: The pain is caused by the position of your arms when you work on the computer.
Señora Díaz: ¿Ah, sí?	Señora Díaz: Really?
Doctor: Sí. Debe apoyar los brazos en la mesa cuando trabaja en la computadora.	Doctor: Yes. You have to rest your arms on the table while working on the computer.
Señora Díaz: Gracias, Doctor.	Señora Díaz: Thank you, doctor.
Doctor: Adiós, señora Díaz.	Doctor: Good bye, Mrs. Díaz.
Señora Díaz: Adiós.	Señora Díaz: Good bye.

3. Reading Comprehension of Cultural Theme

This is the story of Little Red Riding Hood and the wolf's cunning trick to gobble her up with her grandmother. As you know, Little Red Riding Hood knew something was amiss when her grandma's eyes, ears, and mouth looked different than usual.

Había una vez una niña que se llamaba Caperucita Roja.	Once upon a time, there was a little girl called Little Red Riding Hood.
Un día fue a visitar a su abuela.	One day, she went to visit her grandmother.
Salió de su casa y entró en el bosque.	She left her house and went into the woods.
En el bosque se encontró con el lobo.	In the woods, she met the wolf.
—¿Adónde vas Caperucita Roja?	—Where are you going, Little Red Riding Hood?
—Voy a la casa de mi abuela.	—I'm going to my grandma's house.
—Ah, qué bien.	—Oh, that's great.
El lobo corrió por el bosque hasta llegar a la casa de la abuela.	The wolf ran through the forest until he got to the grandmother's house.
El lobo entró y se comió a la abuela.	The wolf went in and ate the grandmother up.
Después el lobo se puso el pijama de la abuela y se metió en la cama.	Then the wolf put the grandmother's pajamas on and got into her bed.

Cuando llegó Caperucita, encontró al lobo en la cama de la abuelita.	When Little Red Riding Hood arrived, she found the wolf in her grandmother's bed.
—¡Qué ojos tan grandes tienes! —dijo Caperucita al lobo.	—What big eyes you have! —said Little Red Riding Hood.
—Para verte mejor —dijo el lobo.	—The better to see you with —said the wolf.
—¡Qué orejas tan grandes tienes! —dijo Caperucita al lobo.	—What big ears you have! —said Little Red Riding Hood.
—Para escucharte mejor —dijo el lobo.	—The better to hear you with — said the wolf.
—¡Qué boca tan grande tienes! —dijo Caperucita al lobo.	—What big mouth you have! — said Little Red Riding Hood.
—Para comerte mejor —dijo el lobo.	—The better to eat you with —said the wolf.
El lobo saltó y se comió a Caperucita.	The wolf jumped and ate Little Red Riding Hood up.
Pero un cazador entró en la casa.	But a hunter went into the house.
Cortó la barriga del lobo y rescató a la abuela y a Caperucita.	He cut the wolf's belly open and rescued the grandmother and Little Red Riding Hood.
El lobo salió corriendo.	The wolf ran away.

| La abuela abrazó a Caperucita. | The grandmother hugged Little Red Riding Hood. |
| Y se sentaron a tomar el té. | And they sat down for tea. |

Let's practice

A. Complete the sentences by choosing one of the words listed below.

ojos - orejas - pijama - boca - abuela - cazador - lobo - Caperucita Roja - casa - bosque

1. Caperucita iba (was going) a casa de su (her) _____.

2. Caperucita se encontró (met) con el _____.

3. El lobo entró en (went in) la _____ de la abuela.

> The story uses both **abuela** and **abuelita**. They both mean the same. Diminutive endings in Spanish are used to express love or affection.

4. El lobo ve mejor (sees better) con los _____.

5. La casa de la abuela estaba (was) en el _____.

6. El lobo escucha mejor (hears better) con las _____.

7. El _____ rescató (rescued) a Caperucita Roja y su abuela.

8. _____ se encontró (met) con el lobo en el bosque.

9. El lobo se puso (put on) el _____ de la abuela.

10. La _____ del lobo era muy grande (was very big).

B. Put these sentences in order:

- El cazador entró en la casa

- La abuela abrazó a Caperucita.

- Caperucita salió de su casa y entró en el bosque.

- El lobo entró y se comió a la abuela.

- Caperucita se encontró con el lobo.

- El lobo saltó y se comió a Caperucita.

- El cazador cortó la barriga del lobo y rescató a la abuela y a Caperucita.

- La abuela y Caperucita se sentaron a tomar el té.

- El lobo salió corriendo.

- Caperucita encontró al lobo en la cama de la abuelita.

4. Grammar Concept: Present Tense of Ser (*to be*)

In English, only one verb means *to be*. We say, for example:

The cake **is** *good.* (description)

The cake **is** *on the table.* (location)

In both cases, the verb is **the same** for describing or pointing out a location.

In Spanish, there is a difference.

The cake **is** *good* can be translated as *La torta* **es** *rica*

but *The cake* **is** *on the table* is *La torta* **está** *sobre la mesa.*

As you see, in one case, we used the verb **ser** (*to be*), and in the other, we used **estar** (also *to be*!).

In Spanish, two verbs mean *to be*: **ser** and **estar**. Let's start with the first one, **ser**. We've already learned the 3rd person singular of ser — **es** — (Fourth Lesson).

> Speaking of pronouns, **usted** is a formal *you*, **ustedes** is the plural (*you all*). **Vosotros** is the same as **ustedes**, but used only in Spain. It means *you all*.

Check this dialogue out:

En la ciudad

JOSÉ: Disculpe, ¿esta **es** la biblioteca?

LUISA: Perdón, no **soy** de aquí.

JOSÉ: Ah, ¿de dónde **es** usted?

LUISA: **Soy** de otra ciudad. No **soy** de Bogotá.

JOSÉ: Ah, **es** turista, como yo.

LUISA: Sí, **soy** turista. Soy de los Estados Unidos. ¿Y usted?

JOSÉ: **Soy** de México.

LUISA: Ah. **Somos** dos turistas. Aquella señora **es** colombiana. Ella **es** de acá.

Glossary:

De aquí: *from here*

¿De dónde…?: *Where… from?*

Otra: *another*

Como: *like*

Acá: *here*

---

		ser to be		
Yo	**soy**	nosotros/as	**somos**
Tú	**eres**	vosotros/as	**sois**
Usted		ustedes	
Él	**es**	ellos	**son**
Ella		ellas	

Uses of ser: The verb **ser** is used in ten basic situations:

1. *To describe*

Yo **soy** rubia = *I am blond*

Tú **eres** alto = *You're tall*

Él **es** joven = *He is young*

Ella **es** inteligente = *She is intelligent*

> **Tip:** Note that in Spanish, you do not need to add the pronoun to a sentence — unless you want to stress it — because it is already included in the verb: **somos** simpáticos (*we are nice*)

149

Somos nietos = *We are grandchildren*

Vosotros **sois** solteros = You all are single

Ustedes **son** románticos = You all are romantic

Ellos **son** morenos = *They are dark-haired*

2. *To indicate a profession or occupation*

Marcos **es** cocinero = *Marcos is a chef*

Yo **soy** estudiante = *I am a student*

Ella **es** médica = *She is a doctor*

Somos cazadores = *We are hunters*

Sois profesores = *You are professors*

> **Tip**: Unlike English, Spanish omits the indefinite article **un/una** before an unmodified profession. For example: **Ellas son doctoras**. But if you modify the profession, you need to add the indefinite article: **Ellas son unas doctoras excelentes.**

Ustedes **son** pilotos = *You are pilots*

Ellos **son** ingenieros = *They are engineers*

3. *To indicate where someone comes from*

Yo **soy** de los Estados Unidos = I am from the United States

Tú **eres** de Colombia = *You are from Colombia*

Él **es** de San Francisco = *He is from San Francisco*

Usted **es** de Francia = *You are from France*

Nosotros **somos** de Nápoles = *We are from Naples*

Vosotros **sois** de Canadá = *You all are from Canada*

Ellos **son** de Irlanda = *They are from Ireland*

4. ***To identify specific features about a person, such as relationship, nationality, race, or religion***

Yo **soy** cristiano = *I am Christian*

Tú **eres** peruano = *You are Peruvian*

Él **es** asiático = *He is Asian*

Somos casados = *We are married*

Vosotros **sois** amigas = *You are friends*

Marcos y Luisa **son** colegas = *Marcos and Luisa are colleagues*

5. To ***say what material something is made of***

La cama **es** de hierro = *The bed is of iron (The bed is made of wood)*

La casa **es** de madera = *The house is of wood (The house is made of wood)*

La silla **es** de plástico = *The chair is of plastic (The chair is made of plastic)*

Los zapatos **son** de cuero = *The shoes are of leather (The shoes are made of leather)*

Las ventanas **son** de vidrio = *The windows are of glass (The windows are made of glass)*

151

6. To *say who something belongs to*

El auto **es** de María = *The car is of María (The car belongs to Maria)*

Las manzanas **son** de Pedro = *The apples are of Pedro (The apples belong to Pedro)*

> **Tip: de + el = del.** When **de** (*of*) is followed by **el** (*the*), the words contract to **del** (*of the*)

El abrigo **es** del muchacho = *The coat is of the boy (The coat belongs to the boy)*

La mano **es** de ella = *The hand is of her (The hand belongs to her)*

La moto **es** de ellos = *The motorcycle is of them (The motorcycle belongs to them)*

7. To say *for whom or for what something is intended*

El pollo **es** para ella = *The chicken is for her*

El vino **es** para ellos = *The wine is for them*

La flor **es** para mi hermana = *The flower is for my sister*

8. To *describe where an event takes place*

El cumpleaños **es** en la casa de María = *The birthday party is in Maria's house*

La ceremonia **es** en la universidad = *The ceremony is at the university*

9. To *make generalizations*

El bosque **es** peligroso = *The forest is dangerous*

10. To *express time, dates, and days of the week.*

Son las 4.00 p.m. = It's 4.00 p.m.

Es el 21 de octubre = It's October 21st

Es lunes = It's Monday

> **Tip:** Note that in Spanish, the days of the week and the months of the year are NOT capitalized like in English.

Let's Practice

A. Where are these famous people from? Use the 3rd person singular of **ser** *(to be)* to say where they're from and their nationality. Remember that countries are capitalized, but not nationalities!

Inglaterra (*England*)   Francia (*France*)   España (*Spain*)

Italia (*Italy*)   Colombia (*Colombia*)   México (*Mexico*)

los Estados Unidos (*the United States*)   Alemania (*Germany*)

Example: Lionel Messi: <u>Es de Argentina. Es argentino.</u>

1. Leonardo da Vinci _____

2. Marie Curie _____

3. Barack Obama _____

4. Albert Einstein _____

5. Frida Khalo _____

6. Pablo Picasso _____

7. Shakira _____

8. Paul McCartney _____

B. Complete the following sentences with the appropriate form of **ser** and include between parentheses *why* you're using this verb: Example: Caperucita Roja es_buena. (description)

- Description

- Profession or occupation

- To indicate nationality

- To indicate relationship

- Material something is made of

- Possession

- For whom something is intended

- Generalizations

- Where an event takes place

- Time, date, or day of the week

1. Mick Jagger _____ inglés (_____)

2. Los suéteres _____ de lana (_____)

3. Caperucita _____ la nieta de la abuela (_____)

4. La torta (cake) _____ para la abuela (_____)

5. _____ martes (_____)

6. Marcos y Luis _____ cazadores (_____)

7. La fiesta de cumpleaños ___ en el parque (_____)

8. La casa _____ de la abuela (_____)

9. El bosque _____ peligroso (_____)

10. El lobo _____ malo (_____).

5. Communication Tips

You're on a trip to a Spanish-speaking country, and a strange flu takes over you. You go to the nearest drugstore to find some medicine that will make you feel better. Here are some helpful questions in case you have any of these symptoms!

Farmacéutico: Buenos días. ¿Cómo puedo ayudarle?	Pharmacist: Good morning. How can I help you?
Cliente: Me siento muy mal.	Client: I feel terrible.
Farmacéutico: ¿Qué síntomas tiene?	Pharmacist: What symptoms do you have?
Cliente: Tengo fiebre.	I have a fever.
Farmacéutico: Le doy ibuprofeno.	Pharmacist: I'll give you some ibuprofen.

Cliente: También tengo dolor de garganta.	Client: I also have a throat ache.
Farmacéutico: Le doy unas pastillas.	Pharmacist: I'll give you some lozenges.
Cliente: Además tengo un resfrío.	Client: I also have a cold.
Farmacéutico: Le doy un descongestivo.	Pharmacist: I'll give a decongestant.
Cliente: Y me duele todo el cuerpo.	Client: And my whole body aches.
Farmacéutico: Para eso haga reposo.	Pharmacist: Get some rest for that.
Cliente: Gracias.	Client: Thank you.
Farmacéutico: De nada. Que mejore.	Pharmacist: You're welcome. Get better.

6. Answer Key

2.

A. Label parts of the body

1. el pelo   4. el hombro

2. la cara/la mejilla   5. el pecho

3. el cuello   6. el ombligo

7. el estómago

8. el pubis

9. el muslo

10. la rodilla

11. la pantorrilla

12. el tobillo

13. el pie

14. el brazo

15. el codo

16. el antebrazo

17. la muñeca

18. la mano

Label parts of the face

1. la frente

2. la ceja

3. la pestaña

4. el ojo

5. la nariz

6. la boca/el labio

7. la oreja

8. el mentón

C.

1. falso

2. verdadero

3. verdadero

4. falso

5. verdadero

6. falso

7. falso

8. falso

9. verdadero

10. falso

11. falso

12. verdadero

D.

ojo - eye	estómago - stomach
boca - mouth	cintura - waist
oreja - ear	muñeca - wrist
nariz - nose	codo - elbow
cabello - hair	rodilla - knee
cara - face	tobillo - ankle
cuello - neck	talón - heel
hombro - shoulder	dedo gordo del pie - toe
espalda - back	cadera - hip
pecho - chest	muslo - thigh

E.

1. Tiene que tomarse la temperatura
2. Tiene que tomar una aspirina
3. Tiene que tomar agua
4. Tiene que hacer reposo
5. Tiene que tomar un antibiótico
6. Tiene que hacer una dieta especial
7. Tiene que ponerse una tirita
8. Tiene que ponerse una inyección de cortisona

3.

A.

1. abuela	6. orejas
2. lobo	7. cazador
3. casa	8. Caperucita
4. ojos	9. pijama
5. bosque	10. boca

B.

1. Caperucita salió de su casa y entró en el bosque.

2. Caperucita se encontró con el lobo.

3. El lobo entró y se comió a la abuela.

4. Caperucita encontró al lobo en la cama de la abuelita.

5. El lobo saltó y se comió a Caperucita.

6. El cazador entró en la casa.

7. El cazador cortó la barriga del lobo y rescató a la abuela y a Caperucita.

8. El lobo salió corriendo.

9. La abuela abrazó a Caperucita.

10. La abuela y Caperucita se sentaron a tomar el té.

4.

A.

1. Leonardo da Vinci es de Italia. Es italiano.

2. Marie Curie es de Francia. Es francesa.

3. Barack Obama es de los Estados Unidos. Es estadounidense.

4. Albert Einstein es de Alemania. Es alemán.

5. Frida Kahlo es de México. Es mexicana.

6. Pablo Picasso es de España. Es español.

7. Shakira es de Colombia. Es colombiana.

8. Paul McCartney es de Inglaterra. Es inglés.

B.

1. Mick Jagger es inglés (to indicate nationality).

2. Los suéteres son de lana (material something is made of).

3. Caperucita es la nieta de la abuela (to indicate relationship).

4. La torta es para la abuela (for whom something is intended).

5. Es martes (day of the week).

6. Marcos y Luis son cazadores (occupation).

7. La fiesta de cumpleaños es en el parque (where an event takes place).

8. La casa es de la abuela (possession).

9. El bosque es peligroso (generalization).

10. El lobo es malo (description).

CHAPTER 7

CHECKING IN: A HOTEL ADVENTURE

1. Cultural Theme: Hospitality in Spanish-speaking Countries

Nowadays, hospitality practices are standardized worldwide. Nevertheless, you might notice a difference when arriving in a Spanish-speaking country vs. an English-speaking one. In English-speaking countries, hospitality emphasizes professionalism and efficiency. No doubt, hotel managers and Airbnb hosts are friendly and attentive. Still, you'll soon notice hospitality is even warmer and more personal in Spain and Latin America, where people try from the beginning to build rapport and form a deeper connection with guests. Service providers may engage in more casual conversation and physical gestures of warmth, such as hugs and kisses on the cheek. Also, English-speaking cultures value direct communication and clarity in verbal and written interactions. This straightforwardness may come across as too direct for a Spanish-speaking traveler who is used to more indirect and nuanced communication. In Spanish-speaking countries, communication requires at least a few minutes of meaningless banter to loosen up and get into the rhythm of things. Not to mention that non-verbal cues and subtleties in language are important and communicate as much information as clear, direct language. So, on your next trip, come with a dose of patience and a repertoire of friendly phrases to break the ice and communicate you're a happy customer!

2. Vocabulary

a. Hotel vocabulary

el hotel	hotel
el hotel de lujo	luxury hotel
el hotel tres estrellas	three-star hotel
el hotel del aeropuerto	airport hotel
el hotel boutique	boutique hotel
el albergue	hostel
alojamiento	lodging
el hostal	hostel
la casa de huéspedes	guest house
la pensión	bed and breakfast
pensión completa	room and full board (all meals)
media pensión	room with breakfast and one other meal
la fecha de llegada	arrival date
la fecha de salida	departure date
en efectivo	in cash

con tarjeta de crédito	with credit card
el código de reserva	reservation code
el hostal	hostel
la casa de huéspedes	guest house
el/la huésped	guest
la recepción	front desk
desocupado	vacant, unoccupied, free
el horario de check-in/check-out	check-in/check-out
la llave	key
la tarjeta	card
la caja de seguridad	safe deposit box
el pasaporte	passport
el nombre completo	full name
el número de teléfono	telephone number
la tarifa de la habitación	room rate
el servicio de habitación	room service
el botones	bellhop
las escaleras	staircase
el ascensor	elevator
el vestíbulo (lobby)	lobby
el restaurante	restaurant
la cafetería	coffee shop
el bar	bar
el gimnasio	gym
la piscina	swimming pool

el estacionamiento	parking lot
el estacionamiento de cortesía	complimentary parking

b. House Vocabulary

la casa	house
el apartamento	apartment
la sala	living room
el sofá	sofa/couch
el sillón	armchair
la mecedora	rocking chair
el cojín	cushion
la mesa de centro	coffee table
la mesa de arrime	side table
la librería	bookcase
la estantería	bookshelf
el perchero	coat rack
el reloj	clock
la alfombra	rug
la chimenea	fireplace
el cuadro	painting
la cortina	curtain
el ventilador	fan
el aire acondicionado	air conditioner
la calefacción	heating
la luz	light

la planta	plant
el comedor	dining room
el aparador	sideboard
la mesa	table
la silla	chair
la habitación/el cuarto	bedroom
la habitación para una persona	single room
la habitación matrimonial	double room
la habitación con/sin baño	room with (out) bathroom
la cama	bed
la sábana	sheet
el acolchado	bedspread
la mesa de luz	nightstand
el escritorio	desk
la lámpara	lamp
el clóset/al armario	closet
la cocina	kitchen
el horno	stove
el fregadero	sink
la nevera/el frigorífico/la heladera	refrigerator
el baño	bathroom
el inodoro	toilet
la ducha	shower
el lavabo	sink

el corredor	hallway
la puerta	door
la ventana	window
el jardín	garden
el patio	patio
el techo	roof

c. Verbs Related to Hospitality

viajar	to travel
quedarse	to stay
confirmar la reserva	to confirm the reservation
cancelar la reserva	to cancel the reservation
con buenas vistas	with good views
ir	to go
hay	there is/there are
reservar	make reservations
confirmar	to confirm
tener	to have
enviar	to send

Let's practice

A. Complete the following words related to the hospitality world according to the description.

1. Caja para guardar (to keep) dinero (money): c_ _ _ de _ _
   g _ _ _ _ _ d

167

2. Lugar para estacionar autos: _ s _ _ _ _ _ _ _ _ _ _ _ o

3. Lugar para hacer gimnasia: g _ _ n _ _ _ o

4. Número para reservar habitaciones en el hotel: c _ _ _ _ o
   de _ e _ _ _ _ a

5. Instrumento para abrir (to open) puertas: ll _ _ _

6. Sistema de transporte vertical: a _ _ _ _ _ _ r

7. Acción de pedir (ask) que el hotel guarde (to keep) una
   habitación: r _ _ _ _ _ _ r

8. Acción de decirle al hotel que no se usará (won't use) la
   habitación: _ a _ _ _ _ _ r

9. Habitación con desayuno y otra comida: m _ _ _ a p _ n
   _ _ _ _

10. Pagar con billetes: Pagar con e _ _ _ _ _ _ o

B. Draw a line from the following objects to the place they
   belong to in the house. Of course, some items may go in
   more than one place!

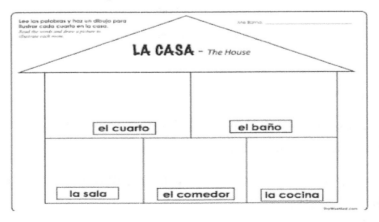

168

el sofá	la cama
el horno	la mesa
la mesa de centro	la chimenea
la mesa de luz	el escritorio
el fregadero	el lavabo
la silla	el inodoro
la lámpara	el perchero
la ducha	el sillón
el techo	el aparador
el frigorífico	

C. Complete this narration with the right word. Check the vocabulary list if you need to remind yourself of the meaning!

Hotel	media pensión	habitación
confirmar	pensión	baño
reservar	enviar	buenas vistas
huéspedes	ducha	la fecha de llegada

Cuando uno viaja al extranjero (when you travel abroad), es importante 1_____ un correo electrónico (an email) para 2_____ una 3_____ en un alojamiento y avisar (let them know) 4_____. En un 5_____ , las habitaciones tienen 6_____ privado con 7_____. En una 8_____, el baño se comparte con otros 9_____, pero se puede tener 10_____ para comer ahí. Es importante pedir (to ask) tener una habitación con 11_____, para (to) disfrutar (enjoy) el

169

paisaje (the landscape). También hay que recordar (you should remember) 12 _____ la reserva para no perderla (so you don't lose the reservation!).

Diálogo I

Making a reservation over the phone:

Sr. Pérez: Buenos días.	Mr. Pérez: Good morning.
Recepcionista de hotel: Buenos días, señor.	Front desk clerk: Good morning, sir.
Sr. Pérez: Quiero hacer una reservación, por favor.	Sr. Pérez: I want to make a reservation, please.
Recepcionista: Perfecto.	Clerk: Perfect.
Sr. Pérez: ¿Tiene habitaciones disponibles?	Sr. Pérez: Do you have available rooms?
Recepcionista: Sí, tenemos. ¿Para cuántos huéspedes?	Clerk: Yes, we do. For how many guests?
Sr. Pérez: Resérveme una habitación para cinco personas, por favor.	Sr. Pérez: Book me a room for five, please.
Recepcionista: Por supuesto.	Clerk: Sure thing.
Sr. Pérez: Gracias. Adiós.	Sr. Pérez: Thank you. Goodbye.

Diálogo II

At the reception desk.

Huésped: Buenos días. Tengo una reserva a nombre de Juan López.	Guest: Good morning. I have a reservation under the name of Juan López.
Recepcionista: Bien. Para cinco huéspedes, ¿verdad?	Clerk: That's right. It's for five guests, ¿right?
Huésped: Así es.	Guest: That's it.
Recepcionista: ¿Me permite su identificación, por favor?	Clerk: May I have your ID, please?
Huésped: Aquí tiene.	Guest: Here you are.
Recepcionista: Thank you.	Clerk:Thank you.
Huésped: ¿A qué hora es el desayuno?	Guest: What time is breakfast?
Recepcionista: Es de siete a nueve de la mañana.	Clerk: It's from seven to nine in the morning.
Huésped: Gracias.	Guest: Thank you.
Recepcionista: Que tenga una buena estadía.	Clerk: Have a pleasant stay.

Dialogue III

Finding out about hotel amenities

Huésped: Tengo algunas preguntas, por favor.	Guest: I have some questions, please.
Recepcionista: Sí, por supuesto.	Clerk: Yes, of course.
Huésped: ¿El ascensor lleva a la piscina?	Guest: Does the elevator take me to the pool?
Recepcionista: Sí, señor. Marque el menos dos.	Clerk: Yes, sir. Press minus too.
Huésped: Gracias. ¿A qué hora abre el gimnasio?	Guest: What time does the gym open?
Recepcionista: Abre a las ocho de la mañana.	Clerk: It opens at eight in the morning.
Huésped: ¿La habitación tiene caja de seguridad?	Guest: Does the room have a safe deposit box?
Recepcionista: Sí, está dentro del clóset.	Clerk: Yes, it's inside the closet.
Huésped: ¿Hay servicio de lavandería?	Guest: Do you have laundry service?
Recepcionista: Sí, tenemos.	Clerk: Yes, we do.

Huésped: ¿Y tienen servicio de habitación?	Guest: And do you have room service?
Recepcionista: Sí, tenemos servicio de habitación.	Clerk: Yes, we do.
Huésped: Muchas gracias.	Guest: Thank you very much.
Recepcionista: De nada, señor.	Clerk: You're welcome, sir.

3. Reading Comprehension of Cultural Theme

This song is by the Argentine singer, songwriter, and multi-instrumentalist Charly García. In this song, instead of using the verbal form **puedes** (*you can*), he uses **podés** because Argentines use the voseo, which is the use of the pronoun **vos** for the second person singular, instead of **tú**. Remember that **podés** (you can) is the same as **puedes** (you can).

https://www.youtube.com/watch?v=ldgUatPszek

Podés pasear en limousine	You can ride a limousine
Cortar las flores del jardín	Cut the flowers in the garden
Podés cambiar el Sol	You can change the Sun
Y esconderte si no quieres verme	And hide if you don't want to see me
Puedes ver amanecer	You can watch the sunrise
Con caviar desde un hotel	With caviar from a hotel

Y no tienes un poquito de amor para dar	And you don't have a little love to give
Yendo de la cama al living	Going from the bed to the living room
Sientes el encierro	You can feel the imprisonment
Yendo de la cama al living	Going from the bed to the living room
Podés saltar de un trampolín	You can jump from a trampoline
Batir un record en patín	Break a speed skating record
Podés hacer un gol	You can score a goal
Y podés llevarte tu nombre al cielo	And you can take your name to heaven
Puedes ser un gran campeón	You can be a great champion
Jugar en la selección	Play in the national team
Y no tienes un poquito de amor para dar	And you don't have a little love to give
Yendo de la cama al living	Going from the bed to the living room
Sientes el encierro	You can feel the imprisonment
Yendo de la cama al living	Going from the bed to the living room
Oh no no no	Oh, no no no
No hay ninguna vibración	There is no vibration

Aunque vives en mundo de cine	Even though you live in the cinema world
No hay señales de algo que vive en mí	There are no signs of something living inside me
Yendo de la cama hasta el living	Going from the bed to the living room
Siento el encierro	I can feel the imprisonment
Voy yendo de la cama hasta el living	I'm going from the bed to the living room

4. Grammar Concept: Present Tense of Estar (to be)

As we said in the previous chapter, the verb *to be* in English works as **ser** and **estar** in Spanish. We say, for example:

The house **is** *white* (description), and you say **La casa es blanca in Spanish.**

The house **is** *in the city* (location) is **La casa está en la ciudad.**

Estar is used to express <u>four basic concepts</u>:

- location: ella **está** en la casa (*she is in the house*)

- health: él **está** enfermo (*he is sick*)

- changing mood or condition: **estoy** feliz (*I am happy*)

- personal opinion: la comida **está** deliciosa (*the food is delicious*)

4 3 4 3 3 3

En el parque

MARÍA: ¿Dónde **está** Felipe?

CLARA: **Está** en su casa.

MARÍA: ¿Por qué?

CLARA: Porque **está** enfermo.

MARÍA: ¿Cómo **está**?

CLARA: **Está** de mal humor.

MARÍA: Sí, qué lástima. El día **está** muy lindo.

Glossary:

Estar de mal humor: *To be in a bad mood.*

Qué lástima: What a shame

This is the present tense of the verb **estar**

estar *to be*			
Yo	**estoy**	nosotros/as	**estamos**
Tú	**estás**	vosotros/as	**estáis**
Usted		ustedes	
Él	**está**	ellos	**están**
Ella		ellas	

When using estar for location, use the preposition en + the article (el, la/los, las): Sara está en la casa.

Here are some more adjectives to use with estar:

contento: happy

de buen humor: in a good mood

enfermo: sick

triste: sad

cansado: tired

Common Mistake: Since English speakers only have one verb (*to be*) to express all these situations, it's normal to be confused about when to use each in Spanish.

Don't say: **Ella está inteligente**. X

The right way to say it is: **Ella es inteligente.** ✓ (description).

Don't say: **Él es en el colegio**. X

The right way to say it is: **Él está en el colegio** (location)

Many adjectives can be used with either **ser** or **estar**, depending on what you want to say. But as a rule, **ser** is used for unchangeable qualities (**soy rubia**), and **estar** is used for changeable qualities (**estoy triste**).

Common Mistake:

177

Ser is used to express a person's **inherent** qualities:

Luisa es cariñosa. Luisa has a sweet-loving character. That's why she's basically lovely.

Estar is used to express a **transitory** condition: **Luisa está cansada.** Luisa is tired now, but she won't be after she rests.

Don't say: **Luisa está cariñosa** (she's not a sweet-loving character on occasions; she's always sweet-loving) or **Luisa es cansada** (she's momentarily tired, not permanently).

Don't say: **Yo soy cansado.** X Say: **Yo estoy cansado.** ✓

Don't say: **Mi papá es en el supermercado.** X Say: **Mi papá está en el supermercado.**✓

Don't say: **Él está un doctor.** X Say: **Él es un doctor.** ✓

Let's practice

4.

A. Write the appropriate form of **estar**. Say why you chose that option:

- location
- health
- changing mood or condition
- personal opinion.

1. Segovia y Bilbao _____ en España (_____)

2. José _____ enfermo (_____)

3. Yo _____ triste. (_____)

4. Juan _____ en la casa. (_____)

5. Nosotros _____ en el barco. (_____)

6. El ajo (garlic)_____ delicioso (_____)

7. Ustedes _____ contentos. (_____)

8. Tú _____ de buen humor. (_____)

B. Now, see if you can tell what verb to use, **ser** or **estar**, according to the meaning of each sentence, and match the verb to the subject in person and number.

Example: María y Juan <u>están</u> tristes.

1. La mesa y las sillas _____ sucias.

2. Él _____ doctor.

3. Nosotros _____ cansados.

4. _____ importante estudiar.

5. Martín y Luis _____ inteligentes.

6. El café _____ para la mujer.

7. La ciudad _____ hermosa.

8. Yo _____ feliz.

9. El sándwich _____ delicioso.

10. Tú _____ una turista.

11. Yo _____ de Buenos Aires.

12. La lección _____ fácil.

13. El niño _____ en el colegio.

14. Ustedes _____ contentos.

15. Nosotros _____ italianos.

16. Sara _____ triste.

17. La torre Eiffel ____ en París.

18. Pedro ____ enfermo.

19. Ellos ____ amigos.

20. Las ventanas ____ de vidrio.

And just as a reminder, we include the verb **ser** (to be) again (see Chapter 6 for a full explanation), so you can check the box when you do exercise C below, which involves both **ser** and **estar**.

Ser *to be*			
Yo	**soy**	nosotros/as	**somos**
Tú	**eres**	vosotros/as	**sois**
Usted		ustedes	
Él	**es**	ellos	**son**
Ella		ellas	

C. Make complete sentences using the appropriate form of **ser** or **estar** + the words between parentheses.

Example: ¿La abuela? (enferma) <u>La abuela está enferma</u>

180

1. ¿Tomás? (español)

   _____

2. ¿El restaurante? (cerrado)

   _____

3. ¿Las hijas de Pedro? (abogadas)

   _____

4. ¿El problema? (muy fácil (very easy))

   _____

5. ¿El libro? (interesante)_____

6. ¿Tú? (furioso)_____

7. ¿La banana? (amarilla)

   _____

8. ¿Nosotros? (interesantes)

   _____

9. ¿La foto? (en la silla)

   _____

5. Communication Tips

Timekeeping can vary significantly across the Spanish-speaking world due to cultural, historical, and regional differences. For example, punctuality norms vary across different Spanish-speaking countries. Unlike cultures such as Germany or the United States, where being on time is a form of respect for other people's time and commitments, and arriving late to appointments or events is considered rude, there is a more relaxed attitude towards being on time in many Spanish-speaking countries. In fact, arriving on the dot to a dinner party or a wedding may highly inconvenience hosts!

Telling Time: ¿Qué hora es?

In Spanish, you use the verb ser (to be) when saying what time it is. If the time is one o'clock or anything between one and two, we use **es la...(es la una).** We use the plural **son las...** (**son las tres**) for all other hours.

Examples

It's one o'clock. – *Es la una.*

It's two o'clock. – *Son las dos.*

It's three o'clock. – *Son las tres.*

It's four o'clock.– *Son las cuatro.*

It's five o'clock. – *Son las cinco.*

It's six o'clock. – *Son las seis.*

It's seven o'clock. – *Son las siete.*

It's eight o'clock. – *Son las ocho.*

It's nine o'clock. – *Son las nueve.*

It's ten o'clock. – *Son las diez.*

It's eleven o'clock. – *Son las once.*

It's twelve o'clock. – *Son las doce.*

Other useful expressions:

de la mañana................... a. m., in the morning

de la tarde......................p. m., in the afternoon de la noche.............................p.m. in the evening

en punto...................................exactly, on the dot, sharp

¿a qué hora?........................... at what time?

a la una (las dos…)................ at 1:00 (2:00…)

del mediodía.................... noon

de la madrugada/de la medianoche........ midnight

Don't confuse **Es/Son la(s)** with **A la(s)**. The first is used for telling time: **Son las** cinco. The second tells when something happens: **La comida es a las ocho de la noche.**

Examples

Son las cuatro de la tarde en punto	It's exactly 4:00 p.m.
¿A qué hora es el desayuno?	At what time is breakfast?
El almuerzo es a las doce de la mañana	Lunch is at 12 a.m.
El viaje es a la una de la tarde	The trip is at 1:00 p.m.

From the hour to the half-hour, Spanish, like English, expresses time by adding minutes or a portion of an hour to the hour. For example, Ten fifteen is **Las diez y quince** or **las diez y cuarto.**

Spanish usually expresses time from the half-hour to the hour by subtracting minutes or part of an hour from the next hour. For example, A quarter to eleven is **Las once menos cuarto.**

When referring to noon or midnight hours, add **del mediodía** if it's noon or **de la medianoche** if it's midnight.

Examples

6:20 a.m.	Son las seis y veinte de la mañana.
11.50 p.m.	Son las doce menos diez de la noche
1:45 p.m.	Son las dos menos cuarto.
12: 20 p.m.	Son las doce del mediodía
7: 35 a.m.	Son las ocho menos veinticinco
5:10 p.m.	Son las cinco y diez
8:25 a.m.	Son las ocho y veinticinco
12: 30 a.m.	Son las doce y media de la madrugada

Let's practice

A. Write down the correct time for each clock.

1. _____

2. _____

3. _____

4. _____

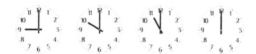

5. _____

6. _____

7. _____

8. _____

9. _____

10. _____

11. _____

12. _____

Keep doing the same with these, and round the time to the nearest number. For example, if it's three thirty-four, write **Son las cuatro menos veinticinco**.

13. _____

14. _____

15. _____

16. _____

17. _____

18. _____

19. _____

20. _____

21. _____

B. ¿Qué hora es? Write the time adding de la mañana, de la tarde or de la noche according to the a.m. or p.m. indicated.

   1. 1:00 a.m.

2. 4. 6:15 p.m.

3. 7. 11:45 a.m. exactly

4. 9:20 p.m.

5. 5. 7:45 a.m.

6. 8. 9:10 p.m. on the dot

7. 11:00 a.m.

8. 6. 4:15 p.m.

9. 9. 9:50 a.m.

C. You're asking the concierge at your hotel when these activities occur. He answers according to the cue. Example: el almuerzo: 12:00 p.m. $\Longrightarrow$ ¿A qué hora es el almuerzo? Es a las doce del mediodía.

1. El desayuno: 8:30 a.m.

2. La cena: 8:00 p.m.

    _____

3. El concierto en el lobby: 10:15 p.m.

    _____

4. La clase de gimnasia (the gym class): 5:20 p.m.

    _____

5. La sesión de masajes (the massage session): 7:00 p.m.

    _____

6. Answer Key

2.

A.

1. caja de seguridad	6. ascensor
2. estacionamiento	7. reservar
3. gimnasio	8. cancelar
4. código de reserva	9. media pensión
5. llave	10. efectivo

B. el cuarto: la cama - la mesa de luz - el escritorio - la silla - el perchero - la lámpara

el baño: el lavabo - la ducha - el inodoro

la sala: el sofá - la mesa de centro - la chimenea - el sillón - el perchero - la lámpara

el comedor: la mesa - la silla - el aparador

la cocina: el horno - el fregadero - el frigorífico

techo: roof

C.

1. enviar	4. La fecha de llegada
2. reservar	5. hotel
3. habitación	6. baño

7. ducha

8. pensión

9. huéspedes

10. media pensión

11. buenas vistas

12. confirmar

4.

A.

1. están (location)

2. está (health)

3. estoy (changing mood or condition)

4. está (location)

5. estamos (location)

6. es (personal opinion)

7. están (changing mood or condition)

8. estás (changing mood or condition)

B.

1. están

2. es

3. estamos

4. es

5. son

6. es

7. es

8. soy

9. es or está (depending on what you want to say)

10. eres

11. soy

12. es

13. está

14. están

15. somos

16. está

17. está

18. está

19. son

20. son

C.

1. Tomás es español.

2. El restaurante está cerrado

3. Las hijas de Pedro son abogadas.

4. El problema es muy fácil.

5. El libro es interesante

6. Tú estás furioso

7. La banana es amarilla

8. Nosotros somos interesantes

9. La foto está en la silla

5.

A.

1. Es la una

2. Son las dos

3. Son las tres

4. Son las cuatro

5. Son las nueve

6. Son las diez

7. Son las once

8. Son las doce

9. Son las cinco

10. Son las seis

11. Son las siete

12. Son las ocho

13. Son las tres menos diez

14. Son las cuatro menos veinticinco

15. Son las cuatro y diez

16. Son las cinco y diez

17. Son las siete menos cinco

18. Son las siete y cuarto

19. Son las ocho y media (or Son las nueve menos veinticinco)

20. Son las nueve y cinco

21. Son las diez y veinte

B.

1. Es la una de la mañana

2. Son las nueve y veinte de la noche

3. Son las once de la mañana

4. Son las seis y cuarto de la tarde

5.Son las ocho menos cuarto de la mañana

6. Son las cuatro y cuarto de la tarde

7. Son las doce menos cuarto de la mañana en punto

8. Son las nueve y diez de la noche en punto

9. Son las diez menos diez de la mañana

C.

1. ¿A qué hora es el desayuno? Es a las ocho y media de la mañana.

2. ¿A qué hora es la cena? Es a las ocho de la noche.

3. ¿A qué hora es el concierto en el lobby? Es a las diez y cuarto de la noche.

4. ¿A qué hora es la clase de gimnasia? Es a las cinco y veinte de la tarde.

5. ¿A qué hora es la sesión de masajes? Es a las siete de la tarde.

CHAPTER 8

WEATHER AND CLIMATE

1. Cultural Theme: A Wide Range of Climate Zones Across the Spanish-speaking work

There is a common misconception that Spain and countries in Latin America have warm, sunny climates year-round. Although this is undoubtedly the case in countries near the equator, like Ecuador and Colombia, which tend to be hot and humid, there are plenty of rather cold areas in the Spanish-speaking world. For example, the southern part of Argentina and Chile has extended periods of freezing weather, which becomes increasingly so towards the south, in areas such as Tierra del Fuego, due to its proximity to Antarctica. Latin America is a large and geographically diverse continent with many climates. You can find extreme cold in the south of Chile and Argentina, humid hot in the Amazon jungle, dry hot in the deserts of Chile, very wet in El Chocó, Colombia, and more. Meanwhile, Spain also offers a wide range of climate areas, from the Mediterranean's sunny beaches to the Pyrenees' snowy peaks, with the dry continental climate in central Spain and the lush, humid regions in northern Cantabria.

2. Vocabulary

el alba	dawn
el frío	the cold
el calor	the heat/hot
la temperatura	temperature
el tiempo	weather
el clima	climate
el viento	wind
la neblina	fog
la bruma	fog
la nube	cloud
la lluvia	rain
el granizo	hail
la tormenta	storm
la tempestad	storm
el temporal	rough weather
el relámpago	lightning
el trueno	thunder
la inundación	flood
el temblor	tremor
la escarcha	frost
el cielo	sky
el sol	sun
la puesta de sol	sunset
la luna	moon
las estrellas	stars

Expressions about time and weather

While in English, we use the verb *to be* to speak about the weather (*it's cold/it's hot*), in Spanish, there are three verbs (in the 3rd person singular) to talk about the weather:

- **hacer** (to do, to make): used for a general description of the weather: **hace frío** (it's cold).

- **estar** (to be): used for specific weather conditions: **está lloviendo** (it's raining), **está ventoso** (it's windy).

- **haber** (to have): also used for particular weather conditions: **hay viento** (it's windy).

Review how to conjugate **hacer, estar**, and **haber**:

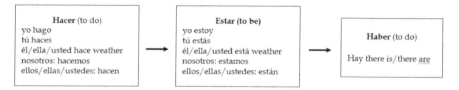

Hacer (to do)
yo hago
tú haces
él/ella/usted hace weather
nosotros: hacemos
ellos/ellas/ustedes: hacen

Estar (to be)
yo estoy
tú estás
él/ella/usted está weather
nosotros: estamos
ellos/ellas/ustedes: están

Haber (to do)
Hay there is/there are

¿Qué tiempo hace?

In Spanish, **tiempo** refers both to weather and to chronological time. In English, we have a different word for each: *weather* (tiempo) and *time* (tiempo).

hacer:

hace frío	it's cold
hace **mucho** frío	it's very cold
hace calor	it's hot
hace **mucho** calor	it's very hot

hace fresco	it's cool
¿Qué tiempo hace?	what's the weather like?
hace buen tiempo	the weather is good
hace mal tiempo	the weather is bad

haber:

hay (mucho) viento	there's (a lot of) wind
hay (mucho) sol	there's (a lot of) sun
hay neblina	it's foggy
hay nubes	it's cloudy
hay polvo	it's dusty

estar

está ventoso	it's windy
está nublado	it's cloudy
está despejado	it's clear
está lloviendo	it's raining
está nevando	it's snowing
está soleado	it's sunny
está húmedo	it's humid
está frío	it's cold
está caluroso	it's hot

Other expressions:

llueve	it's raining
nieva	it's snowing
es árido	it's arid
es húmedo	it's humid
hay contaminación	there's pollution

Idioms with tener (*to have*) and estar (*to be*)

In Spanish, you use the verb **tener** (to have) to express whether you're cold or warm.

tener (mucho) frío	to be (very) cold
tener (mucho) calor	to be (very) warm
estar bien	to be fine

Las estaciones (The seasons)

la primavera	spring
el verano	summer
el otoño	fall
el invierno	winter

Los días de la semana (The days of the week)

lunes	Monday
martes	Tuesday
miércoles	Wednesday

jueves	Thursday
viernes	Friday
sábado	Saturday
domingo	Sunday
el fin de semana	the weekend
por la tarde	in the afternoon
por la mañana	in the morning

Los meses del año (The months of the year)

enero	January
febrero	February
marzo	March
abril	April
mayo	May
junio	June
julio	July
agosto	August
septiembre	September
octubre	October
noviembre	November
diciembre	December

La fecha (The date)

¿Cuál es la fecha de hoy?	What is today's date?
Hoy es el primero de noviembre	Today is November the 1st
Hoy es el diez de marzo	Today is March the 10th

The ordinal number **primero** is used to express the first day of the month: **el primero de diciembre** (December the 1st). For the rest of the days, you use cardinal numbers: **dos, tres, cuatro, cinco, etc.: el tres de marzo** (March the 3rd).

Before the date, you use the definite article **el: el cuatro de abril** (April the 4th).

However, when including the day of the week, **el** is omitted: **Hoy es lunes, cinco de mayo** (Today is Monday, May the 5th).

Let's practice

2.

A. Use one of the expressions below to complete each sentence:

hace frío	hace calor	llueve mucho	es árido
nieva	el clima es tropical	hay viento	hay sol
está nublado	hay mucha contaminación	hace mal tiempo	es húmedo

1. En la Patagonia _____

2. En el desierto del Sahara _____

3. En el Polo Ártico _____

4. En los Andes _____

5. En las Bahamas _____

6. En el Amazonas _____

7. En Ecuador _____

8. En Ciudad de México _____

9. Si (if) hay un temporal, _____

10. Cuando no hay sol, _____

11. En Londres _____

12. En el norte de Brasil _____ todo el año (all year).

B. Say what the weather is like according to what each person wears. You can go back to Chapter 5 to review clothing items.

Example: Chicago: Roberto lleva un suéter, pantalones y abrigo: <u>Hace frío.</u>

1. Cancún: Elena lleva traje de baño y sandalias:

   _____

2. Vail, Colorado: Pedro lleva una chaqueta y pantalones de esquí: _____

3. San Diego: Luisa lleva pantalones cortos y una camiseta: _____

4. Bogotá: Tomás lleva impermeable, botas y tiene un paraguas: _____

5. Río de Janeiro: Silvia lleva un sombrero grande:

   _____

6. Teresa lleva un pantalón, un suéter y una chaqueta:_____

C. Sebastián is from Santiago de Chile and is moving to the United States. His friend Pedro explains what the weather is like in some cities in the U.S.

Use the time expressions you learnt: hace frío - hace calor - llueve mucho - es árido - hay viento - hay mucho sol - hay mucha contaminación - nieva mucho. Example: En Seattle <u>llueve</u>.

En Arizona _____   En Los Ángeles _____

En Seattle _____   En Miami _____

En Chicago _____   En Hawái _____

En California _____   En Syracuse, NY _____

D. Express these dates in Spanish. Example: January 7: <u>el siete de enero.</u>

a. August 2   d. May 3   g. July 4

b. December 1   e. June 10   h. March 18

c. February 20   f. January 12   i. October 6

E. Complete the following weather expressions with **hacer, estar,** or **haber** in the third person singular (**hace, está,** or **hay**) (see above for verbs).

1. _____ mucho calor.

2. _____ mucho viento.

3. _____ nevando.

4. _____ sol.

5. ¿Qué tiempo _____?

6. _____ mal tiempo.

7. _____ neblina.

8. _____ nublado.

9. _____ frío.

10. _____ nevando.

Dialogue I

María: ¿Cuál es tu estación favorita?

María: What's your favorite season?

Pedro: El otoño es mi estación favorita.

Pedro: Fall is my favorite season.

María: ¿El otoño? ¿Por qué?

María: Fall? Why?

Pedro: Porque hace calor de día y está fresco de noche.

Pedro: Because it's warm during the day and it's cool at night.

María: Mi estación favorita es la primavera.

María: My favorite season is spring.

Pedro: ¿Por qué?

Pedro: ¿Why?

María: Porque me gustan las flores.

María: Because I love flowers.

Dialogue II

Teresa: ¿Qué tiempo hace?	Teresa: What is the weather like?
Raúl: Hace mal tiempo.	Raúl: The weather is terrible.
Teresa: ¿Hace frío?	Teresa: Is it cold?
Raúl: No hace frío, pero está lloviendo.	Raúl: It's not cold, but it's raining.
Teresa: ¿Llueve mucho?	Teresa: Is it raining a lot?
Raúl: Sí, hay una tormenta fuerte.	Raúl: Yes, there's a terrible storm.
Teresa: ¿Hay truenos y relámpagos?	Teresa: Is there thunder and lightning?
Raúl: Sí, hay truenos muy fuertes.	Raúl: Yes, the thunder is very loud.
Teresa: Por suerte, el pronóstico dice que mañana hará buen tiempo.	Teresa: Luckily, the forecast says tomorrow the weather will be nice.

3. Reading Comprehension of Cultural Theme

This is the story of the ugly duckling and how he is forced to survive a winter by himself when the other birds shun him for being unattractive (the story is in the present tense to make it easier to understand). The following spring, the duckling discovers something remarkable about himself.

En un estanque, una mamá pato tiene seis patitos.	In a pond, a mother duck has six ducklings.
Todos los patitos son amarillos.	All the ducklings are yellow.
Pero un patito es gris y feo.	But one duckling is gray and ugly.
Los patitos amarillos desprecian al patito feo.	The yellow ducks shun the ugly duckling.
En el invierno, los patitos abandonan al patito feo.	In winter, the ducks abandon the ugly duckling.
El patito feo está solo.	The ugly duckling is all by himself.
Hace mucho frío.	It's very cold.
Nieva y hay mucho viento.	It snows and it's very windy.
El patito tiene mucho frío.	The duckling is very cold.
Necesita refugiarse.	He needs to find refuge.
Se refugia en un granero.	He takes refuge in a barn.
Allí pasa todo el invierno.	He spends the whole winter there.
Finalmente, llega la primavera.	Finally, spring arrives.
Sale el sol y hace buen tiempo.	The sun comes out, and the weather is good.

El patito feo regresa al estanque.	The ugly duckling goes back to the pond.
Mira hacia abajo.	He looks down.
Y observa su reflejo en el agua.	And sees his reflection in the water.
¡Qué sorpresa!	What a surprise!
¡Es un cisne hermoso!	He's a beautiful swan!

Let's practice

A. Join the first part of the sentence on the left with the correct ending on the right:

1. En el invierno   sale el sol

2. Los patitos amarillos   un precioso cisne

3. El patito tiene mucho frío   observa su reflejo en el agua

4. El patito feo es   en el invierno

5. En la primavera   hace mucho frío

6. Cuando el patito mira hacia abajo   desprecian al patito feo

B. Fill in the crossword puzzle.

Across

3. ¿Cuántos patitos tiene la mamá pato?

5. Estación del año cuando hace frío.

7. Elemento que forma un estanque.

8. El patito feo observa una imagen en el _____.

9. En el invierno hace _____.

Down

1. En el otoño el _____ sopla fuerte.

2. En el invierno _____.

4. En la _____ salen flores (flowers bloom).

6. El patito feo se refugia (takes refuge) en un _____.

4. Grammar Concept

1. Pronouns

A pronoun is a word used in place of a noun. For example, in the following sentence, *she* replaces *Sue*: *She* is skating on the pond. *She* is a pronoun. Here is a list of pronouns in Spanish:

yo	I
tú (*inf.*)	you
usted (*form.*)	you
él ella	he she
nosotros nosotras	we
vosotros vosotras	you all

ustedes	you all
ellos ellas	they

In Latin American Spanish, **ustedes** is the plural of both **usted** and **tú** — **vosotros** is not used. Every time you address a group of people, whether the relationship is formal or informal, you use **ustedes**. Its abbreviation is **Uds**.

In Spain, instead of **ustedes**, they use **vosotros** as the plural of **tú**. The form **vosotros** is only used in Spain.

In Spanish, the pronoun **usted** (you) is used for formal relationships: your boss, a stranger, a salesperson, the cashier at the bank. You use it when you meet someone for the first time. Its abbreviation is **Ud**. (always with a capital **U**).

Instead, the pronoun **tú** (you) is used for informal relationships: your friends and family.

The masculine plural form **ellos** refers to a group of males or a group that includes both males and females.

Instead, the feminine plural form **ellas** relates only to a group of females.

Did you know? In Spanish, there is no subject pronoun **it**. This unique feature adds a fascinating twist to your language-learning journey. You use **él** and **ella** to refer to people and sometimes animals. But when it comes to things, they have their own way of being referred to.

Let's practice

A. What would you say with each of the following, **tú** or **usted**?

Your grandmother: ___   A professor: _____

A coworker: _____   A repair person: ____

A flight attendant: _____   Your cousin: _____

Your boss: _____   Your best friend: ____

II. Expressing Actions: Verbs ending in -ar

Throughout this workbook, we have already used many Spanish verbs in their conjugated form. And you've done great at "deciphering" their meaning in context. Now it's time to really tackle each group. This will help you understand how they work and master them yourself!

What is a *conjugated form*? It's when the verb adopts a form that matches the subject it refers to. For example, in *I speak*

Spanish, speak has that form because it reflects the subject doing the action (*I*); in *he speaks Danish, speaks* has that form because the person doing the action is a *he*. All Spanish verbs are conjugated by adding a personal ending to the verb's stem that reflects the subject doing the action. For example, in the verb **hablar, habl-** is the stem to which you add the endings **-o, -as, -a, -amos, -áis, -an** depending on who is doing the action. These endings belong to the present tense.

Remember, when we talk about *infinitives*, we refer to the action by itself, with no reference to who is doing it or when. In English, the infinitive is indicated by *to*: *to run, to play, to jump*. In Spanish, all infinitives end in **-ar, -er,** and **-ir**. We will start with infinitives ending in **-ar**. Examples of these verbs are:

bailar (to dance)	buscar (to look for)	desear (to want)
hablar (to talk)	cantar (to dance)	enseñar (to teach)
caminar (to walk)	comprar (to buy)	estudiar (to study)
necesitar (to need)	pagar (to pay for)	practicar (to practice
regresar (to come back)	tomar (to take; to drink)	trabajar (to work)
esquiar (to ski)	jugar (to play)	nadar (to swim)
tocar (to play)	preparar (to prepare)	abandonar (to abandon)
pasar (to spend)	llegar (to arrive)	mirar (to look)

> In Spanish, the meaning of *for* is included in the verbs **pagar** (*to pay for*) and **buscar** (*to look for*). Don't say *yo pago para* or *yo busco para*.

The **present tense** form of verbs ending in -**ar** is conjugated by removing the infinitive -**ar** ending and replacing it with an ending corresponding to the person performing the action of the verb. See below:

hablar *to speak*			
Yo	**habl-o**	nosotros/as	**habl-amos**
Tú	**habla-s**	vosotros/as	**habl-áis**
Usted		ustedes	
Él	**habl-a**	ellos	**habl-an**
Ella		ellas	

As for how to turn a sentence into a negative, just place the word **no** before the conjugated verb: **Ella no habla español** (*She doesn't speak Spanish*).

Let's practice

A. Complete the table using the correct verb form.

	hablar	buscar	cantar	comprar	pagar	hablar	necesitar	trabajar
yo	hablo				pago		necesito	
tú		buscas				hablas		
él/ella/ usted			canta					trabaja
nosotros	hablamos			compramos			necesitamos	
vosotros		buscáis		compráis	pagáis			
ellos/ellas/ ustedes			cantan			hablan		trabajan

B. Give the correct **subject pronoun** according to the verb. Example: hablo: <u>yo</u>

1. _____ bailamos	4. _____ caminas	7. _____ trabajo
2. _____ necesitas	5. _____ regresa	8. _____ enseñamos
3. _____ compramos	6. _____ toman	9. _____ estudia

C. Complete these sentences with the correct verb form to match the person doing the action.

1. Mi abuelo _____ (trabajar) los sábados.

2. En el verano nosotros _____ (tomar) sol.

3. Tú _____ (mirar) la nieve por la ventana.

4. Ella _____ (enseñar) en la universidad.

5. Yo ____ (viajar) a España en febrero.

6. Martín _____ (comprar) zapatos en Italia.

7. Tus hijos _____ (buscar) un programa de televisión.

8. La profesora _____ (explicar) el problema.

9. La señora _____ (pagar) la cuenta en el restaurante.

10. Yo _____ (necesitar) una cartera negra.

D. Complete the following paragraph with the correct form of the infinitives.

María y Pedro son personas muy ocupadas (very busy). Los lunes 1._____ (trabajar) en la oficina. Los martes 2._____ (comprar) la comida en el supermercado. Los miércoles 3._____ (estudiar) en la universidad. Los jueves 4. _____ (trabajar) en su casa. Los viernes 5._____ (caminar) diez kilómetros (kilometres). Los sábados por la mañana 6._____ (limpiar) la casa y 7._____ (cocinar) para el resto de la semana (for the rest of the week). Los sábados por la tarde 8._____ (nadar) en una piscina. Los domingos 9. _____ (descansar) y 10._____ (escuchar) música clásica (classic music).

5. Communication Tips

It's essential to know how to express preferences when you travel. You already learned how to express when you like or dislike something: **Me gusta** _____ (I like _____) and **No me gusta** _____ (I don't like _____) or how to ask someone else if they like or dislike something: **¿Te gusta__?** or **¿Le gusta___?** (Do you like _____?) or how to talk about a third person: **¿Le gusta** _____? (¿Does he like _____?). We also learned that you can pair the infinitive form with **me gusta** and **no me gusta**

213

(**me gusta comer chocolates**: *I like eating chocolates*). In this chapter we have learned the verbs **necesitar** (*to need*) and **desear** (*to want*). These verbs can also be paired with infinitives: **Necesito comprar pan** (*I need to buy bread*) and **Deseo regresar a España** (*I want to return to Spain*). Now, we will add two other verbs to express preferences that can also be followed by infinitives. For now, we will only learn the **yo** forms:

quiero + infinitive (I want to + infinitive)	⟹	**quiero comprar zapatos**
prefiero + infinitive (I prefer to + infinitive)	⟹	**prefiero tomar agua**

6. Answer Key

2.

A.

1. En la Patagonia hay viento.

2. En el desierto del Sahara es árido.

3. En el Polo Ártico hace frío.

4. En los Andes nieva.

5. En las Bahamas hay sol.

6. En el Amazonas es húmedo.

7. En Ecuador el clima es tropical.

8. En Ciudad de México hay mucha contaminación.

9. Si hay un temporal, hace mal tiempo.

10. Cuando no hay sol, está nublado.

11. En Londres llueve mucho.

12. En el norte de Brasil, hace calor todo el año.

B.

1. Hace calor.

2. Está nevando.

3. Hace calor.

4. Llueve.

5. Hay sol.

6. Hace frío.

C.

En Arizona es árido.	En Los Ángeles hay mucha contaminación.
En Seattle hace frío.	En Miami hace calor.
En Chicago hay viento.	En Hawái llueve mucho.
En California hay mucho sol.	En Syracuse, NY nieva mucho.

D.

a. el dos de agosto	c. el tres de mayo	e. el cuatro de julio
b. el primero de diciembre	d. el diez de junio	f. el dieciocho de septiembre

E.

1. Hace mucho calor.

2. Hay mucho viento.

3. Está nevando.

4. Hay sol.

5. ¿Qué tiempo hace?

6. Hace mal tiempo.

7. Hay neblina.

8. Está nublado.

9. Hace frío.

10. Está nevando.

3.

A.

1. En el invierno hace mucho frío.

2. Los patitos amarillos desprecian al patito feo.

3. El patito tiene mucho frío en el invierno.

4. El patito feo es un precioso cisne.

5. En la primavera sale el sol.

6. Cuando el patito mira hacia abajo observa su reflejo en el agua.

B.

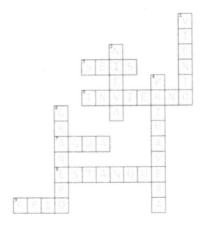

4.

I.

Cuando el patito mira hacia abajo observa su

Your grandmother: tú	A professor: usted
A coworker: tú	A repair person: usted
A flight attendant: usted	Your cousin: tú
Your boss: usted	Your best friend: tú

II.

A.

	hablar	buscar	cantar	comprar	pagar	hablar	necesitar	trabajar
yo	hablo	busco	canto	compro	pago	hablo	necesito	trabajo
tú	hablas	buscas	cantas	compras	pagas	hablas	necesitas	trabajas
él/ella/ usted	habla	busca	canta	compra	paga	habla	necesita	trabaja
nosotros	hablamos	buscamos	cantamos	compramos	pagamos	hablamos	necesitamos	trabajamos
vosotros	habláis	buscáis	cantáis	compráis	pagáis	habláis	necesitáis	trabajáis
ellos/ellas/ ustedes	hablan	buscan	cantan	compran	pagan	hablan	necesitan	trabajan

B.

1. nosotros bailamos	4. tú caminas	7. yo trabajo
2. tú necesitas	5. él/ella/usted regresa	8. nosotros enseñamos
3. nosotros compramos	6. ellos toman	9. él/ella/usted estudia

C.	D.
1. trabaja	1. trabajan
2. tomamos	2. compran
3. miras	3. estudian
4. enseña	4. trabajan
5. viajo	5. caminan
6. compra	6. limpian
7. buscan	7. cocinan
8. explica	8. nadan
9. paga	9. descansan
10. necesito	10. escuchan

CHAPTER 9

HIKING AND THE NATURAL WORLD

1. Cultural Theme: Exploring Nature in Spanish-speaking Countries

Senderismo is the word for hiking in Spanish, and it's one of the most preferred activities in these countries, attracting millions of visitors every year to its beautiful landscapes. This time, it may be you who feels like planning a trip to explore nature in a Spanish-speaking country. And it's a good idea. Spain and Latin America offer diverse hiking environments, from lush rainforests to challenging mountains. The most striking trekking is in Patagonia, where you can explore places like El Chaltén, a hikers' haven in southern Argentina, with trails starting almost on your hostel's doorstep, or Torres del Paine, in Chile, known for its dramatic granite peaks, glaciers, and turquoise lakes. If you want to experience a unique destination, the Perito Moreno glacier in Santa Cruz, Argentina, is where you'll want to head. Considered the world's eighth wonder, this imposing ice mass is a spectacle few will want to miss. For a more lush experience, plan to hike the Inca trail in Perú, leading you through the heart of the Peruvian Andes to the ancient city of Machu Picchu. As for discovering natural beauty in Spain, Picos de Europa, located in northern Spain, offers dramatic limestone peaks and deep gorges to explore, and the Sierra Nevada in southern Spain provides diverse hiking trails with views of the Mediterranean Sea.

2. Vocabulary

el senderismo	hiking
el sendero	trail
el senderista	hiker
el camino	path
la caminata	the walk
la escalada	the climb
el atajo	shortcut
el valle	valley
el arroyo	stream
el arroyo de montaña	mountain stream
el río	river
el lago	lake
la laguna	lagoon
la cascada	waterfall
el barranco	ravine
el acantilado	cliff
la sierra	hill
la colina	hill

la cadena de montañas	mountain range
la cordillera	mountain range
la montaña	mountain
la ladera	slope
la cima	summit/top of the mountain
la cumbre	summit/top of the mountain
el pico	peak
la cota	mark
la cueva	cave
el bosque	forest
el árbol	tree
la roca	rock
el medio ambiente	environment
el pájaro	bird
el puente colgante	suspension bridge
el campamento base	base camp
el punto de partida o fin de la caminata	trailhead
el guía	guide
el guardaparque	park ranger
el itinerario	itinerary
la flecha	arrow
la mochila	backpack
las botas	boots
el sombrero	hat

la gorra	cap
el calzado para senderismo	hiking footwear
las botas/los zapatos de trekking	hiking boots or hiking shoes
la carpa	tent
la brújula	compass
la navaja	pocket knife
la cuerda	rope
la olla	pot
la cantimplora	water bottle
la botella de agua	water bottle
las bolsas de residuos	garbage bags
el bastón de trekking	cane
la caña de pescar	fishing pole
la canoa	canoe
la bolsa/el saco de dormir	sleeping bag
la manta	blanket
el botiquín	first aid kit
la linterna	flashlight
los fósforos	matches
la fogata	campfire
el fuego	fire
la leña	firewood
los binoculares	binoculars
la cámara de fotos	camera
el agua potable	drinking water

el mapa	map
el mosquitero	mosquito net
el repelente	repellent
el protector/bloqueador solar	sunblock
los anteojos de sol	sunglasses
la capa de lluvia	rain poncho

Verbs

hacer senderismo	to go hiking
escalar	to climb
caminar	to walk
hacer trekking	to do trekking
saltar	to jump
cruzar	to cross
trepar	to climb up
bajar	to climb down
llevar	to take
guardar	to keep
cavar	to dig
subir	to go up/to climb
pescar	to fish
remar	to row
cortar	to cut
nadar	to swim
andar a caballo	to horseback ride

Let's practice

A. Guess what? Each of these things is used for something when you go camping. **Se usa para...** (you use it for...). Guess what it is.

1. Se usa para guardar cosas y se lleva en la espalda: _____

2. Se usa para protegerse (to protect) los pies al caminar: _____

3. Se usa para dormir (sleep): _____

4. Se usa para llevar agua: _____

5. Se usa para orientarse (to get one's bearings): _____

6. Se usa para protegerse (to protect oneself) de la lluvia: _____

7. Se usa para prender (to light) el fuego: _____

8. Se usa para cortar: _____

9. Se usa para ver (to see) de lejos (from afar): _____

10. Se usa para sacar fotos: _____

11. Se usa para iluminar (to light up) un lugar (a place): _____

12. Se usa para curar (to cure) heridas (wounds): _____

B. Say which word doesn't belong in the group:

1. los fósforos - la fogata - la cantimplora - el fuego

2. la capa de lluvia - el mosquitero - la cámara de fotos - el protector solar

3. el puente colgante - el mapa - el guía - el itinerario

4. la montaña - la cueva - la colina - la sierra

5. el lago - el valle - la laguna - el río

6. el sendero - el camino - el atajo - la cascada

7. la brújula - la cuerda - la navaja - la fogata

8. bajar - subir - trepar - escalar

9. el sombrero - la brújula - la gorra - las botas

10. el senderista - el guardaparque - la flecha - el guía

C. Say what you prefer doing. Example: ¿Prefieres hacer trekking o esquiar? <u>Prefiero hacer trekking.</u>

1. ¿Prefieres caminar o escalar?

    _____

2. ¿Prefieres llevar anteojos de sol o gorra?

    _____

3. ¿Prefieres caminar en el bosque o en la montaña?

    _____

4. ¿Prefieres dormir (to sleep) en una cama o en la bolsa de dormir?

    _____

5. ¿Prefieres pescar en (in) la laguna o en el río?

_____

6. ¿Prefieres escalar una montaña o trepar una colina?

_____

D. This is what Luis does every weekend. See if you can conjugate these verbs ending in **-ar** (learned in Chapter 8). As a refresher, see the table below for reference.

hablar *to speak*			
Yo	**habl-o**	nosotros/as	**habl-amos**
Tú	**habla-s**	vosotros/as	**habl-áis**
Usted		ustedes	
Él	**habl-a**	ellos	**habl-an**
Ella		ellas	

Todos los sábados Luis 1_____ (caminar) por la montaña. 2_____ (llevar) una mochila con unos binoculares, protector solar y un mapa. 3_____ (necesitar) conducir hasta la montaña. 4_____ (buscar) un sendero fácil (easy) y 5_____ (trepar) durante dos horas. Siempre (always) 6_____ (tomar) un atajo hasta llegar a la cima. Allí (there) 7_____ (preparar) una fogata y 8_____ (cocinar) unas salchichas para comer. También 9_____ (descansar) y 10_____ (mirar) el paisaje.

11_____ (regresa) a las cinco de la tarde y 12_____ (llegar) a su casa a las seis de la tarde.

Although you probably already recognize some **prepositions** in Spanish, we've been using them all along because it's impossible to write anything without them! Let's go over the ones you'll encounter more frequently. Notice in the paragraph above the prepositions used:

- por la montaña ⟹ through the mountain

- con unos binoculares ⟹ with some binoculars

- hasta la montaña ⟹ as far as the mountains

- durante dos horas ⟹ during two hours

- hasta llegar a la cima ⟹ up to the top

- para comer ⟹ to eat

- a las cinco de la tarde ⟹ at five o'clock

Prepositions

a ....at/to	en...............in/on
ante............... before	entre.......... between
con............... with	hacia........... toward
contra .... against	hasta............until/up to/as far as
de............... of/from	para ....to/for/in order
desde..........after/since/from	por............. by/for/through
durante......... during	sin............. without
sobre...........on/upon/above/over	según........ according to

Contraction **de + el = del**

Contraction **a + el = al**

The contraction only happens with the masculine singular article.

Examples:

Es la casa *del* hombre Salta al lago frío.

El niño salta *al* lago.

Todas las partes *del* mundo.

Juan camina *al* sendero.

E. Write the correct preposition: a - con - de - en - para - durante - sin - hacia - hasta

Felipe y Teresa van 1_____ pescar todos los fines de semana 2 _____ desconectarse de la ciudad. Manejan el auto 3____llegar a un lago y se meten 4____ una canoa 5____ las cañas de pescar. Empiezan 6____ remar 7 _____ el centro del lago, donde hay más peces. Luego pescan 8_____ dos horas 9_____ la hora 10____ almuerzo. Comen unos sándwiches y unas frutas. Después, continúan pescando. A veces, regresan 11___ casa 12____ ningún pescado. Lo importante es relajarse y disfrutar 13____la naturaleza.

Dialogue I

Martín: ¡Qué lindo día!	Martín: What a beautiful day!
Sofía: Vamos a hacer trekking en las montañas.	Sofía: Let's go do some trekking in the mountains.
Martín: ¿Qué llevamos?	Martín: What do we take?
Sofía: Una mochila con repelente de mosquitos, protector solar y el mapa.	Sofía: A backpack with bug repellent, sunblock, and the map.
Martín: ¿Qué comemos?	Martín: ¿What do we eat?
Sofía: Preparo unos sandwiches.	Sofía: I'll prepare some sandwiches.
Martín: ¿Y qué bebemos?	Martín: And what do we drink?

Sofía: Bebemos agua del arroyo.	Sofía: We drink water from the stream.
Martín: Yo llevo los binoculares para observar pájaros.	Martín: I'll take the binoculars to do some bird watching.
Sofía: ¡Buena idea!	Sofía: Good idea!

Diálogo II

María: ¿Te gusta hacer senderismo?	María: Do you like hiking?
Tomás: Sí, me encanta hacer senderismo.	Tomás: Yes, I love hiking.
María: ¿Prefieres trepar montañas o caminar?	María: Do you prefer climbing mountains or walking?
Tomás: Prefiero trepar montañas.	Tomás: I prefer climbing mountains.
María: ¿Por qué?	María: Why?
Tomás: Porque me gusta llegar a la cima.	Tomás: Because I like getting to the top.
María: Sí, en la cima está la mejor vista.	María: Yes, you get the best views on the top of the mountain.
Tomás: Sí, me encanta la sensación de llegar a la cumbre.	Tomás: Yes, I love the feeling of making it to the top.

3. Reading Comprehension of Cultural Theme

«**Caminante, no hay camino**» (*Traveler, there is no path*) is a beautiful poem by Spanish poet Antonio Machado (1875-1939), included in his book *Proverbs and Canticles*. The road is a metaphor for our lives: each person has to find their own way because there are no markings on the road of life. Once a path is trodden, the next person walking on it has to discover things all over again.

Caminante son tus huellas	Traveler, your footprints are
el camino, y nada más;	the path and nothing more;
caminante, no hay camino,	Traveler, there is no path;
se hace camino al andar.	you carve out a path as you go.
Al andar se hace camino,	As you go, you carve a path
y al volver la vista atrás	and when you look back
se ve la senda que nunca	you'll discover a path that you will never
se ha de volver a pisar	travel on again.
Caminante, no hay camino,	Traveler, there is no path;
sino estelas en la mar.	only trails across the sea.

Below is the poem «**Viento, agua, piedra**» (*Wind, water, stone*), which belongs to Mexican poet Octavio Paz (1914-1998). It refers to the cyclical nature of our lives. Like water, wind, and stone, we are simultaneously impacted by those around us.

El agua horada la piedra	Water hollows stone,
el viento dispersa el agua	wind scatters water,
la piedra detiene el viento.	stone stops wind.
Agua, viento, piedra.	Water, wind, stone.
El viento esculpe la piedra,	Wind sculpts stone,
la piedra es copa del agua,	stone is a cup for water,
El agua escapa y es viento	water runs off and is wind.
Piedra, viento, agua.	Stone, wind, water.
El viento en sus giros canta,	Wind sings as it whirls,
el agua al andar murmura,	water murmurs as it flows,
la piedra inmóvil se calla.	the motionless stone is quiet.
Viento, agua, piedra.	Wind, water, stone.
Uno es otro y es ninguno:	One is the other and is neither:

entre sus nombres vacíos	through their vacant names
pasan y se desvanecen	they pass through and disappear
agua, piedra, viento.	water, stone, wind.

4. Grammar Concept

Expressing Actions: Verbs Ending in -er

Now, we will tackle another group of regular verbs: those with infinitive endings in **-er** that follow the pattern of **comer** (*to eat*). Examples of these verbs are:

aprender (to learn)	comer (to eat)	beber (to drink)
comprender (to understand)	creer (to think, to believe in)	leer (to read)
vender (to sell)	meter (to put in)	correr (to run)
deber + infinitive: must, should + infinitive	prender (to turn on)	romper (to break)
esconder (to hide)	leer (to read)	correr (to run)
prender (to turn on)	coser (to sew)	barrer (to sweep)
cometer (to commit)	acceder (to access)	arder (to burn)

The present tense form of verbs ending in **-er** is conjugated by removing the infinitive **-er** ending and replacing it with an ending corresponding to the person performing the action of the verb. See below:

comer *to eat*			
Yo	**com-o**	nosotros/as	**com-emos**
Tú	**com-es**	vosotros/as	**com-éis**
Usted		ustedes	
Él	**com-e**	ellos	**co-men**
Ella		ellas	

Let's practice

Complete the following sentences with the appropriate form of the infinitive between parenthesis.

A.

1. María camina y Tomás _____(correr).

2. Sebastián y yo _____ (prender) una fogata para cocinar las salchichas (hot dogs).

3. Ellos _____ (esconder) sus verdaderas intenciones (their true intentions).

4. Luisa y Raúl ____ (beber) dos litros de agua por día.

5. Tú _____ (comer) demasiada (too much) comida chatarra (junk food).

6. Sara _____ (coser) una media rota.

7. Los ladrones _____ (cometer) un delito (a crime).

8. Nosotros _____ (leer) mucho en nuestra (our) casa.

9. Yo _____ (meter) la torta en el horno.

10. Ustedes _____ (barrer) la cocina todos los días.

11. María _____ (leer) un libro por mes, y Juan _____ (leer) un libro año.

12. El niño _____ (aprender) muy (very) rápido (fast) a leer.

13. Mis abuelos _____ (vender) su casa y _____ (comprar) un departamento.

14. En un concierto, el público _____ (deber) hacer silencio (keep quiet).

15. El joven no _____ (creer) en nada.

16. Ustedes _____ (meter) las bolsas (bags) de supermercado en la casa.

17. Nosotros _____ (comer) comida sana.

18. El niño _____ (romper) el jarrón (the vase) con la pelota (the ball).

19. Tú _____ (vender) tu auto para comprar uno nuevo (a new one).

20. La comida picante (hot food) _____ (arder) en la boca.

B. Give the correct **subject pronoun** according to the verb.
Example: hablo: <u>yo</u>

1. ____ prendemos	5. ____ metes	9. ____ beben
2. ____ escondo	6. ____ corremos	10. ____ arde
3. ____ venden	7. ____ crees	11. ____ leo
4. ____ cosemos	8. ____ barréis	12. ____ comen

C. Complete the table using the correct verb form:

	aprender	comer	beber	prender	leer	correr	comprender	meter
yo	aprendo				leo			
tú			bebes			corres		metes
él/ella/ usted		come		prende		corre		
nosotros							comprende mos	
vosotros			bebéis		leéis			metéis
ellos/ellas/ ustedes	aprenden			prenden				

D. Practicing **-ar** (see chapter 8) and **-er** ending verbs. Change the verbs in this paragraph from the first person plural (nosotros) to the first person singular (yo).

Nosotros <u>tenemos</u> una casa en la montaña. Allí <u>leemos y descansamos</u> los fines de semana. Durante el día (during the day) <u>caminamos</u> por las laderas de la montaña. Por la tarde, <u>andamos</u> a caballo o <u>nadamos</u> en el lago. <u>Comemos</u> muy temprano (very early) por la noche. A veces (sometimes) <u>bebemos</u> vino. Después <u>leemos</u> frente a la chimenea o <u>jugamos</u> un juego (a game). ¡<u>Creemos</u> que (that) es una vida fantástica!

Yo_____

_____

_____

_____

_____

_____

_____

_____

Before doing the next exercise, a reminder: In Spanish, you don't need to express the subject. For example, you can say: **Corre doce kilómetros todos los días** (*He runs twelve kilometres every day*). Notice the **Él** is omitted. Verbs are accompanied by a subject pronoun only for clarification, emphasis, or contrast. For example: **¡Yo no como carbohidratos!** (*I don't eat carbohydrates!*) includes the pronoun to emphasize the speaker's point. Otherwise, it's not as in English, in which a verb must have an expressed subject (a noun or pronoun). So remember, not to write the subject pronoun when doing this exercise!

E. Translate the following:

1. I learn_____

2. She learns_____

3. We insist_____

4. They sell _____

5. You (sing.) eat _____

6. He runs _____

7. They turn on _____

8. It burns _____

9. You (pl.) read _____

10. We put in _____

11. You (pl.) understand _____

12. I think _____

5. Communication Tips

Siete tips para hacer senderismo

Caminar por la naturaleza es una actividad para grandes y pequeños, jóvenes y personas mayores. Se adapta a todas las edades y se practica en cualquier momento del año. Estos son unos consejos para disfrutar más el senderismo.

1. Elegir bien la ruta. Debes elegir bien la ruta: dónde empieza, dónde termina, la distancia y el nivel de dificultad.

2. Llevar siempre un mapa. Llevar un mapa o una aplicación en el móvil para no perderte.

3. Caminar acompañado por alguien. El senderismo es una actividad para practicar con familia o amigos.

4. Llevar ropa y calzado adecuados: suéter y chaqueta para el frío, protector solar contra el sol, zapatos de trekking, una capa de lluvia si hay nubes.

5. Llevar una mochila con todo lo necesario: la botella de agua, el protector solar, la gorra, la chaqueta.

6. Llevar comida y bebida para el camino. Recomendamos fruta, barritas energéticas, frutos secos, nueces, semillas o galletas.

7. Respetar el medio ambiente. No arrojar residuos ni arrancar flores ni ramas.

Glosario:

se adapta: to adapt itself

edades: ages

puede adaptarse y realizarse: It can adapt itself and be done

en cualquier momento del año: any time of the year

unos: some

disfrutar: enjoy

más: more

elegir: choose

bien: well

dónde: where

empieza: starts

termina: ends

distancia: distance

nivel de dificultad: level of difficulty

aplicación: an app

móvil: cell phone

perderte: get lost

acompañado: accompanied

alguien: someone

hacer: to do

adecuados: adequate

si: if

todo: all

lo necesario: necessary things

recomendamos: we recommend

barritas energéticas: energy bars

frutos secos: dried fruits

nueces: nuts

seeds: semillas

galletas: crackers

respetar: to respect

arrojar: to throw

residuos: trash

arrancar: pull out

ramas: branches

6. Answer Key

2.

A.

1. la mochila
2. el calzado para senderismo/las botas/los zapatos de trekking
3. la bolsa o saco de dormir
4. la cantimplora o botella de auga
5. la brújula
6. la capa de lluvia
7. los fósforos
8. la navaja
9. los binoculares
10. la cámara de fotos
11. la linterna
12. el botiquín

B.

1. la cantimplora	6. la cascada
2. la cámara de fotos	7. la fogata
3. el puente colgante	8. bajar
4. la cueva	9. la brújula
5. el valle	10. la flecha

C.

Answers may vary but could be:

1. Prefiero caminar.

2. Prefiero llevar gorra.

3. Prefiero caminar en la montaña.

4. Prefiero dormir en una cama.

5. Prefiero pescar en la laguna.

6. Prefiero trepar una colina.

D.

1. camina	7. prepara
2. lleva	8. cocina
3. necesita	9. descansa
4. busca	10. mira
5. trepa	11. regresa
6. tomar	12. llega

E.

1. a	5. con
2. para	6. a
3. hasta	7. hacia
4. en	8. durante

9. hasta

10. de or del

11. a

12. sin

13. de

4.

A.

1. corre	11. lee/lee
2. prendemos	12. aprende
3. esconden	13. venden/compran
4. beben	14. debe
5. comes	15. cree
6. cose	16. meten
7. cometen	17. comemos
8. leemos	18. rompe
9. meto	19. vendes
10. barren	20.arde

B.

1. nosotros	5. tú	9. ellos/ustedes
2. yo	6. nosotros	10. él/ella/usted
3. ellos	7. tú	11. yo
4. nosotros	8. vosotros	12. ellos/ustedes

C.

	aprender	comer	beber	prender	leer	correr	comprender	meter
yo	aprendo	como	bebo	prendo	leo	corro	comprendo	meto
tú	aprendes	comes	bebes	prendes	lees	corres	comprendes	metes
él/ella/ usted	aprende	come	bebe	prende	lee	corre	comprende	mete
nosotros	aprendemos	comemos	bebemos	prendemos	leemos	corremos	comprendemos	metemos
vosotros	aprendéis	coméis	bebéis	prendéis	leéis	corréis	comprendéis	metéis
ellos/ ellas/ ustedes	aprenden	comen	beben	prenden	leen	corren	comprenden	meten

D. Yo tengo una casa en la montaña. Allí leo y descanso los fines de semana. Durante el día camino por las laderas de la montaña y nado en el lago. Por la tarde, ando a caballo o nado en el lago. Como muy temprano por la noche. A veces bebo vino. Después leo en la sala o juego un juego. ¡Creo que es una vida fantástica!

E.

1. aprendo

2. aprende

3. insistimos

4. venden

5. comes

6. corre

7. prenden

8. arde

9. leéis

10. ponemos

11. comprendéis

12. creo

CHAPTER 10

FITNESS

1. Cultural Theme: The pursuit of fitness in Spanish-speaking countries

R egular exercise is one of the best things you can do for your health. People know this worldwide, but the fitness approach can vary from country to country. As in all other aspects, Spanish-speaking countries have a different attitude towards fitness than their English-speaking counterparts. To begin with, taking care of one's well-being in Spanish-speaking countries is more relaxed, and fitness sessions may occur in public parks and outdoor spaces. In English-speaking countries, there is a stronger emphasis on private fitness facilities. In Spanish-speaking countries, fitness activities often have a social component: men and women exercise with friends and turn a workout session into a social experience. The gym is a great place to meet like-minded people. In Spain and Latin America, group sports and community events are prevalent. In English-speaking countries, the approach is more individualistic. While there certainly are group classes and sports leagues, people are more focused on meeting their fitness goals and attending the next activity on their calendar. Home fitness equipment and digital fitness subscriptions in English-speaking countries also isolate people more in their homes. That said, globalization has made the fitness culture ubiquitous worldwide. Everyone is into looking after their physical appearance and leading a healthy lifestyle. And no matter where you go, someone will always be going for a run at 5 a.m.

2. Vocabulary

el gimnasio	the gym
la gimnasia	gym
los vestuarios	locker room
la piscina	swimming pool
la colchoneta	mat
las pesas	weights
la cinta de correr	treadmill
la press de banca	bench press
las mancuernas	dumbbells
las pesas rusas	kettlebells
la bicicleta fija	exercise bike
los ejercicios	cardio exercises
las sentadillas	squats
los abdominales	sit-ups or crunches
las estocadas	lunges
la flexión de pecho	push-ups
la plancha	plank

la natación	swimming
los músculos	muscles
el abdomen	belly
la espalda	back
el pecho	chest
los glúteos	buttocks
los hombros	shoulders
el cuello	neck
los cuádriceps	quads
el jacuzzi	jacuzzi
el sauna	sauna
la ducha de agua caliente	hot water shower
el spa	spa
los parques públicos	public parks
los espacios al aire libre	outdoor spaces
las clases de gimnasia grupales	group fitness classes
el entrenamiento aeróbico	aerobic training
el HIIT (entrenamiento a intervalos de alta intensidad)	high-intensity interval training
el entrenamiento de fuerza	strength training
el ejercicio	exercise
el circuito de entrenamiento	circuit training
las repeticiones	reps
la serie	series
la rutina	routine

la rutina de ejercicios	workout
el peso	weight
la intensidad	intensity
el precalentamiento	warm up
el relajamiento	relaxation

Verbs

levantar pesas	to lift weights
hacer ejercicios de cardio	to do cardio exercises
hacer gimnasia	to workout
hacer ejercicio	to exercise
hacer ejercicios aeróbicos	to do aerobic exercises
tonificar	to tone
aumentar la masa muscular	to build muscle
subir pulsaciones	to increase heart rate
nadar	to swim
relajarse	to relax
tomar una ducha	to take a shower
correr	to run
andar en bicicleta	to bike
cambiarse	to change

Numbers					
21	veintiuno	30	treinta	40	cuarenta
22	veintidós	31	treinta y uno	50	cincuenta
23	veintitrés	32	treinta y dos	60	sesenta
24	veinticuatro	33	treinta y tres	70	setenta
25	veinticinco	34	treinta y cuatro	80	ochenta
26	veintiseis	35	treinta y cinco	90	noventa
27	veintisiete	36	treinta y seis	100	cien
28	veintiocho	37	treinta y siete	101	ciento uno
29	veintinueve	38	treinta y ocho	199	ciento noventa y nueve
39	treinta y nueve	200	doscientos		

Let's practice

A. Give the correct word according to the definition.

1. Preparación gradual para hacer gimnasia:

    _____

2. Conjunto de repeticiones y series de ejercicios:

    _____

3. Número de repeticiones de un mismo (same) ejercicio:

    _____

4. Lugar donde se practica la natación:

    _____

5. Superficie acolchada (padded) delgada (thin) para recostarse y hacer gimnasia:

_____

6. Herramienta con peso para aumentar la masa muscular de los brazos:_____

7. Acción de ejercitarse: _____

8. Ejercicio que se hace de pie agachándose (squatting) para trabajar los músculos de los muslos, la cadera y los glúteos: _____

9. Máquina para correr en el mismo sitio:

_____

10. Lugar donde se hace gimnasia:

_____

11. Momento de recuperación al final de una rutina:

_____

12. Partes del cuerpo que se trabajan con la gimnasia:

_____

B. Say what exercise each person needs to do for the different parts of the body.

Use the verb **necesitar + usar** (to use), **necesitar + hacer** (to do) or **necesitar + tomar** (to take).

Example: **Para los brazos María necesita usar (I need to use) las pesas** or

Para cambiarse, José necesita usar el vestuario.

And here's a reminder of how to conjugate **necesitar** (an - ar verb):

necesitar *to need*		
Yo **necesit-o**	nosotros/as **necesit-amos**	
Tú **necesit-as**	vosotros/as **necesit-áis**	
Usted	ustedes	
Él **necesit-a**	ellos	**necesit-an**
Ella	ellas	

1. Para las piernas, Carlos _____
2. Para los brazos, María _____
3. Para tener buena salud, tú _____
4. Para el abdomen, nosotros _____
5. Para los muslos, ellos _____
6. Para los glúteos, yo _____
7. Para tonificar todo el cuerpo tú _____
8. Para mejorar la resistencia, él _____
9. Para trabajar todo el cuerpo, nosotros _____
10. Para fortalecer los brazos, ella _____
11. Para socializar, nosotros _____
12. Para mejorar la salud del corazón, yo

_____

C. Let's practice the expressions **me encanta** (I love...) and **prefiero** (I prefer). Write five sentences like the following example with the vocabulary above. Example: **Me encanta levantar pesas pero prefiero nadar** (I love lifting weights but prefer swimming).

1. Me encanta _____ pero prefiero
_____.

2. Me encanta _____ pero prefiero
_____.

3. Me encanta _____ pero prefiero
_____.

4. Me encanta _____ pero prefiero
_____.

5. Me encanta _____ pero prefiero
_____.

Dialogue I

Recepcionista: Buenos días, ¿puedo ayudarla?	Receptionist: Good morning, can I help you?
Cliente: Sí, me gustaría empezar a hacer gimnasia.	Client: Yes, I'd like to start working out.
Recepcionista: ¡Qué buena idea!	Receptionist: That's a great idea!
Recepcionista: ¿Le gusta tomar clases o prefiere la sala de máquinas?	Receptionist: Do you like taking classes or prefer using the gym equipment?
Cliente: Me gustan más las clases.	Client: I like the classes better.

Recepcionista: Tenemos dos tipos de clases: gimnasia aeróbica y gimnasia funcional.	Receptionist: We have two types of classes: aerobic and functional gym.
Cliente: ¿Y cuál es la diferencia?	Client: And what is the difference?
Recepcionista: El ejercicio aeróbico sube el ritmo cardíaco durante un tiempo prolongado a través de una coreografía con música.	Receptionist: Aerobic exercise increases your heart rate for an extended period of time through choreographed steps performed with music.
Cliente: ¿Y el entrenamiento funcional?	Client: ¿And what about functional training?
Receptionist: El entrenamiento funcional trabaja los músculos con ejercicios de peso, fuerza y resistencia.	Receptionist: Functional training exercises muscles with weight, strength, and resistance exercises.
Cliente: Prefiero la gimnasia aeróbica. ¡Me encanta la música!	Client: I prefer aerobic workouts. I love music!

Dialogue II

Alumna: Profesora, ¿cómo hace la plancha?	Student: Teacher, how do you do a plank?
Instructor: Primero, me acuesto boca abajo en el suelo con las manos bajo los hombros.	Instructor: First, I lay face down on the floor with my hands underneath my shoulders.
Instructor: Segundo, se apoyan los dedos de los pies y las manos en el suelo.	Instructor: Second, I rest my toes and hands on the floor.

253

Instructor: Estiro los brazos a la altura de los hombros.	Instructor: I stretch my arms at shoulder level.
Instructor: Aprieto los glúteos y el vientre.	Instructor: I tighten my buttocks and belly.
Instructor: Me quedo en esta posición durante un minuto.	Instructor: I stay in this position for a minute.
Instructor: El cuerpo debe alinearse de la cabeza a los pies como una tabla.	Instructor: The body should align itself from head to toe like a plank.
Alumna: ¡Guau, parece exigente!	Student: Wow, it looks challenging!
Instructor: ¡Con la práctica, se logra fácilmente!	Instructor: You manage to do it easily with practice!

3. Reading Comprehension of Cultural Theme

This is the story of a hare and a rabbit who run a race, proving that being fast doesn't always get you there first. What matters is being perseverant.

Una liebre y una tortuga se encuentran en un camino.	A hare and a turtle meet on a road.
«¿Corremos una carrera hasta el final del camino?», la liebre pregunta a la tortuga.	«Shall we run a race until the end of the road?» the hare asks the turtle.
La liebre confía en ganar la carrera.	The hare trusts she will win the race.
Ella corre mucho más rápido que la tortuga.	She runs much faster than the turtle.

La tortuga acepta.	The turtle accepts.
Empieza la carrera y la liebre sale corriendo muy rápido.	The race starts, and the hare starts running very fast.
La tortuga avanza muy despacio.	The turtle moves forward very slowly.
La liebre le lleva una gran ventaja.	The hare has a huge advantage.
Decide dormir un rato al lado del camino.	She decides to sleep for a while by the side of the road.
Pero duerme profundamente y se olvida de todo.	But she sleeps soundly and forgets about everything.
Mientras tanto la tortuga avanza lenta pero segura.	Meanwhile, the turtle moves forward slowly but surely.
Después de un rato, la tortuga pasa al lado de la liebre, que duerme todavía.	After a while, the turtle walks past the hare, still sleeping.
La tortuga nunca se detiene.	The turtle never stops.
Finalmente, la tortuga llega a la meta.	Finally, the turtle reaches the finish line.
Le gana a la liebre.	She beats the hare.
Todos los animales del bosque la aclaman con entusiasmo.	All the animals in the forest cheer her with excitement.
¡La liebre se despierta y no lo puede creer!	The hare wakes up and can't believe it!
¡La tortuga es la ganadora!	The turtle is the winner!

Let's practice

A. ¿Verdadero o falso?

1. La tortuga corre muy rápido: _____

2. La liebre invita a la tortuga a correr una carrera: _____

3. La tortuga empieza la carrera muy rápido: _____

4. La liebre sale corriendo muy despacio: _____

5. La liebre decide dormir un rato sobre un árbol: _____

6. La tortuga decide almorzar durante la carrera: _____

7. La tortuga pasa al lado de la liebre mientras duerme: _____

8. La liebre gana la carrera: _____

9. Los animales del bosque aclaman a la tortuga: _____

10. La tortuga es la ganadora: _____

B. Let's practice some prepositions! Read the story again and then try to fill in the blanks with the correct preposition without peeking!

These are the prepositions you may use:

a - hasta - con - de - en - hacia - del (de + el) - mientras - al (a + el)

1. La liebre y la tortuga se encuentran _____ el camino.

2. Corren una carrera _____ el final ___ camino.

3. La liebre confía ___ ganar la carrera.

4. La liebre decide dormir ___ lado ____ camino.

5. La liebre se olvida ____ todo

6. La tortuga avanza ___ la meta (the finish line).

7. La tortuga llega ___ la meta.

8. La tortuga le gana ___ la liebre.

9. Los animales aclaman ___ entusiasmo ___ la tortuga.

10. ____ la tortuga camina, la liebre duerme.

4. Grammar Concept

I. Expressing Actions: Verbs Ending in -ir

Next, we will tackle another group of regular verbs with infinitive endings in **-ir** that follow the pattern of **partir** (*to leave*). Examples of these verbs are:

vivir (to live)	abrir (to open)	compartir (to share)
decidir (to decide)	describir (to describe)	escribir (to write)
recibir (to receive)	discutir (to discuss)	subir (to go up)
sufrir (to suffer)	prohibir (to prohibit)	asistir (a) (to attend, go to)
insistir (en) (to insist)	recurrir (to turn to)	existir (to exist)

The present tense form of verbs ending in **-ir** is conjugated by removing the infinitive **-ir** ending and replacing it with an ending corresponding to the person performing the action of the verb. See below:

partir *to leave*			
Yo	**part-o**	nosotros/as	**part-imos**
Tú	**part-es**	vosotros/as	**part-ís**
Usted		ustedes	
Él	**part-e**	ellos	**part-en**
Ella		ellas	

Let's practice

A. Give the corresponding forms. Remember, you don't need to add pronouns!

1. yo (sufrir, insistir, prohibir, subir, abrir)

_____

2. tú (recibir, vivir, subir, escribir, compartir)

_____

3. él (existir, recurrir a, asistir a, escribir, recibir)

_____

4. nosotros (sufrir, decidir, discutir, abrir, escribir)

_____

5. ellos (describir, abrir, vivir, decidir, subir)

_____

B. Form complete sentences based on the cues given, making the necessary changes to make nouns and adjectives agree. Don't use the subject pronoun in the sentences when the subject pronoun is between parentheses. Add the article (el, la, los, las, un, una, un, unos) when necessary, making it agree in gender and number to the noun next to it. Example: **(yo) recibir/mucho/correos electrónicos/por/día. <u>Yo recibo muchos correos electrónicos por día</u>** (I receive many emails every day), or **Él/escribir/libro/por/año. <u>Escribe un libro por año.</u>**

1. niño/abrir/regalo/de/cumpleaños.

2. niña/escribir/carta/a/su/abuela.

3. (yo) asistir/a/función/de/ópera/en/teatro.

4. Ana/partir/a/Italia/para/aprender/italiano.

5. gobierno/prohibir/uso/de/motocicletas/en/
parques/de/ciudad

6. Sofía y Pedro/discutir/sobre/política/cuando/estar/
juntos.

7. perro/compartir/hueso/con/gato.

8. película/describir/historia/María Antonieta.

9. precios/subir/durante/Navidad/por/gran/
cantidad/de/turistas. _____

10. (yo) sufrir/de/calor/en/verano.

_____

C. Complete the table using the correct verb form:

	vivir	abrir	decidir	compartir	escribir	subir	prohibir	recibir
yo	vivo				escribo			
tú			decides			subes		recibes
él/ella/ usted		abre		comparte		sube		
nosotros		abrimos					prohibimos	
vosotros			decidís		escribís		prohibís	recibís
ellos/ellas/ ustedes	viven			comparten				

II. Linking words

When you first start learning a language, you may get the basic structure of a sentence right but fail to speak cohesively like a real native. One of the secret ingredients is the **linking words**. Check out the difference it makes to have a word that links your sentences and makes them flow:

Mary likes chocolate. Peter likes chocolate (without linking words) ⟹Mary likes chocolate, *and* Peter does too.

Or

Mary likes chocolate. Peter doesn't (without linking words) ⟹ Mary likes chocolate, *but* Peter doesn't.

At this point, we will learn only a few linking words (or *conjunctions*) in Spanish:

y (and): Teresa escribe **y** Pedro lee (Teresa writes and Peter reads)

e (and) (used when the word following the linking word starts with an "i" sound): María **e** Inés estudian chino.

ni (nor): No me gusta hacer gimnasia **ni** deportes (I don't like working out nor sports).

o (or):   ¿Caminas **o** corres? (Are you walking or running?)

u (or) (used when the word following the linking word starts with an "o" sound): Llega en taxi **u** ómnibus (She arrives by taxi or bus).

también (also): Yo **también** leo mucho (I also read a lot)

pero (but): Lee alemán, **pero** no lo habla (He reads German, but doesn't speak it)

aunque (although): Trabaja mucho, **aunque** gana poco (He works hard, although he doesn't earn much)

como (like): Cocina bien **como** su madre (She cooks well like her mother).

porque (because): Aprende italiano **porque** vive en Roma (She learns Italian because she lives in Rome)

mientras (while): **Mientras** ella entra, él sale (While she goes in, he comes out)

sino (but, except): No trabaja en una oficina, **sino** en su casa (She doesn't work in an office, but in her house).

Let's practice

A. Fill in the correct linking word in each sentence:

1. Martín _____ su hermano trabajan juntos.

2. ¿Deseas té ___ café?

3. ¿Visitas Francia __ Holanda?

4. _____ prepara la comida, su hija pone la mesa (sets the table).

5. Su oficina no está en el centro, _____ en las afueras (the outskirts) de la ciudad.

6. Mi cumpleaños es el 13 de enero, _____ lo festejo (I celebrate it) el 20 de enero.

7. Me gustan los perros y _____ los gatos.

8. Llegamos tarde _____ hay mucho tráfico (there's a lot of traffic).

9. Hace gimnasia _____ no le gusta.

10. Andrés _____ Inés bailan bien.

11. Prepara el arroz _____ su abuela.

12. No trabaja _____ estudia.

5. Communication Tips: Explaining your reasons

When you're talking with someone, sometimes explaining **why** you did something is necessary. Here are some words that speakers use to offer explanations in Spanish:

porque	because
para	in order to, to
por eso	that's why, for that reason

Let's practice

A. Fill in the blanks with the correct "explanation word"

1. Necesita una computadora _____ trabajar.

2. Asiste a conciertos; _____ conoce mucho de música.

3. Vende los pantalones _____ no los necesita.

4. Desea un perro _____ estar acompañada.

5. Sus padres le hablan en alemán; _____ comprende la lengua (the language).

6. Debe dar el examen _____ necesita pasar el curso (pass the course).

7. Necesita un televisor _____ mirar el partido de fútbol (the football match).

8. Trabaja mucho _____ necesita ahorrar dinero (save money).

9. Mi auto está roto; _____ tomo el tren.

10. Vivo en el centro de la ciudad _____ estar cerca (close) del trabajo (job).

6. Answer Key

1.

A.

1. precalentamiento 2. rutina 3. serie 4. piscina 5. colchoneta 6. mancuerna o pesas rusas 7. hacer ejercicio 8. sentadilla 9. cinta de correr 10. gimnasio 11. relajación 12. músculos

B.

Answers may vary, but here are some suggestions:

1. Para las piernas, Carlos necesita hacer estocadas.

2. Para los brazos, María necesita levantar pesas.

3. Para tener buena salud, necesitas hacer gimnasia.

4. Para el abdomen, necesitamos hacer abdominales (notice you don't use the article **los** when **abdominales** comes right after **hacer**).

5. Para los muslos, necesitan usar la bicicleta fija.

6. Para los glúteos, necesito hacer sentadillas.

7. Para tonificar todo el cuerpo, necesitas hacer la plancha.

8. Para mejorar la resistencia, necesita usar la cinta de correr.

9. Para trabajar todo el cuerpo, necesitamos hacer natación o nadar.

10. Para fortalecer los brazos, necesita hacer ejercicios cardiovasculares.

11. Para socializar, necesitamos tomar clases de gimnasia grupales.

12. Para mejorar la salud del corazón, necesito hacer ejercicios aeróbicos.

C. Answers may vary, but here are some suggestions:

1. Me encanta usar mancuernas, pero prefiero levantar pesas.

2. Me encanta hacer gimnasia en un gimnasio pero prefiero hacer gimnasia en un parque público.

3. Me encanta el entrenamiento aeróbico, pero prefiero el entrenamiento de fuerza.

4. Me encantan las estocadas, pero prefiero los abdominales.

5. Me encantan los ejercicios de glúteos, pero prefiero los ejercicios de brazos.

3.

A.

1. falso 2. verdadero 3. falso 4. falso 5. falso 6. falso 7. verdadero 8. falso 9. verdadero 10. Verdadero

B.

1. en 2. hasta… del 3. en 4. al … del 5. de 6. hacia 7. a 8. a 9. con … a 10. mientras

4.

A.

1. sufro	Insisto	Prohíbo	Subo	abro
2. recibes	vives	subes	escribes	compartes
3. existe	recurre a	asiste a	escribe	recibe
4. sufrimos	decidimos	discutimos	abrimos	escribimos
5. describen	abren	viven	deciden	suben

B.

1. El niño abre el regalo de cumpleaños.

2. La niña escribe una carta a su abuela.

3. Asisto a una función de ópera en el teatro.

4. Ana parte a Italia para aprender italiano (notice it's not **el italiano**).

5. El gobierno prohíbe el uso de motocicletas en los parques de la ciudad.

6. Sofía y Pedro discuten sobre política cuando están juntos.

7. El perro comparte el hueso con el gato.

8. La película describe la historia de María Antonieta.

9. Los precios suben durante la Navidad por la gran cantidad de turistas.

10. Sufro de calor en el verano.

C.

	vivir	abrir	decidir	compartir	escribir	subir	prohibir	recibir
yo	vivo	abro	decido	comparto	escribo	subo	prohíbo	recibo
tú	vives	abres	decides	compartes	escribes	subes	prohíbes	recibes
él/ella/ usted	vive	abre	decide	comparte	escribe	sube	prohíbe	recibe
nosotros	vivimos	abrimos	decidimos	compartimos	escribimos	subimos	prohibimos	recibimos
vosotros	vivís	abrís	decidís	compartís	escribís	subís	prohibís	recibís
ellos/ellas/ ustedes	viven	abren	deciden	comparten	escriben	suben	prohíben	reciben

4.

II

1. Martín y su hermano trabajan juntos.

2. ¿Deseas té o café?

3. ¿Visitas Francia u Holanda?

4. Mientras prepara la comida, su hija pone la mesa (sets the table).

5. Su oficina no está en el centro, sino en las afueras (the outskirts) de la ciudad.

6. Mi cumpleaños es el 13 de enero, pero lo festejo (I celebrate it) el 20 de enero.

7. Me gustan los perros y también los gatos.

8. Llegamos tarde porque hay mucho tráfico (there's a lot of traffic).

9. Hace gimnasia aunque no le gusta.

10. Andrés e Inés bailan bien.

11. Prepara el arroz como su abuela.

12. No trabaja ni estudia.

5.

A.

1. Necesita una computadora para trabajar.

2. Asiste a conciertos; por eso conoce mucho de música.

3. Vende los pantalones porque no los necesita.

4. Desea un perro para estar acompañada.

5. Sus padres le hablan en alemán; por eso comprende la lengua.

6. Debe dar el examen porque necesita pasar el curso.

7. Necesita un televisor para mirar el partido de fútbol.

8. Trabaja mucho porque necesita ahorrar dinero.

9. Mi auto está roto; por eso tomo el tren.

10. Vivo en el centro de la ciudad para estar cerca del trabajo.

KEEPING THE GAME ALIVE

Congratulations on making it to the end of **Spanish Workbook for Adults**! You're now equipped with everything you need to take your Spanish skills to the next level.

But before you go, I have one last request...

Would you pass on your newfound knowledge and show other readers where they can find the same help?

By leaving your honest opinion of this book on Amazon, you'll show other learners where they can find the information they're looking for, and pass your passion for Spanish forward.

Thank you for your help. The love of learning Spanish is kept alive when we share our knowledge – and you're helping us do just that.

Thank you again, and happy learning!

- Your biggest fan, Morelingua Academy

CONCLUSION

Hey there, rockstar linguists!

Can you believe it? From those first uncertain "hola" to confidently chatting away about your favorite "comida," you've come a heck of a long way. You've transformed from absolute beginners to confident Spanish speakers, ready to tackle conversations without the deer-in-headlights look. Pretty awesome, right?

Remember those key takeaways we chatted about? Daily practice (yes, including those tongue-twister days), making Spanish a part of your daily routine (even your dog's learning by osmosis), and using every tool and app under the sun to turn your brain into a Spanish language powerhouse. We dived into the wonderful world of Spanish-speaking cultures, not just to beef up our grammar but to truly connect with the heart and soul of the language. And let's not forget all those real-life applications we talked about—traveling, boosting your career, and making friends across the globe. That's the real treasure at the end of this rainbow.

Reflecting on our cultural immersion, isn't it fascinating how learning Spanish allows us to peek into a world so vibrant and diverse? It's not just about rolling your Rs or mastering subjunctive moods; it's about understanding the stories, the struggles, and the joys of over 500 million people.

And, oh, the places you'll go with Spanish! Whether it's navigating a bustling market in Mexico City, acing a job interview for that multinational corporation, or simply making a new friend, the practical applications of what you've learned are as boundless as they are exciting.

But hey, this isn't "adiós," it's more of an "hasta luego." Consider this the beginning of a lifelong adventure in language and cultural exploration. The world of Spanish is vast and filled with wonders waiting to be discovered by you.

Remember, you're not going at it alone. There's a whole community out there—forums, language exchange partners, social media groups—ready to support you, laugh with you, and grow with you. Dive in, engage, ask questions, and share your experiences. The world is your oyster, or should I say, "el mundo es tu ostra."

I hope this little workbook of ours has sparked a flame of passion for Spanish that will burn brightly for years to come. I believe in you and your ability to achieve fluency, embrace the challenges, and savor the rewards of learning this beautiful language.

I'd love to hear about your journey—your triumphs, your facepalm moments, and everything in between. Your feedback is like gold; it helps make this resource even better for the next wave of Spanish enthusiasts. Drop me a line at [insert contact information or social media handles], or just ping me to say "qué tal."

As we wrap up, I want to leave you with this: Keep exploring, keep learning, and keep opening your heart to new experiences. The beauty of language learning is not just in the words you master but in the worlds you discover along the way.

Here's to endless adventures, in Spanish and beyond. ¡Vamos allá!

Con cariño,

el equipo de MORELINGUA ACADEMY

REFERENCES

- *Evidence-Based Design Principles for Spanish ...*
  https://www.frontiersin.org/articles/10.3389/fcomm.20
  21.639889

- *Spanish Pronunciation with Audio*
  https://studyspanish.com/pronunciation

- *The ultimate guide to Spanish accent marks & how to type ...*
  https://www.berlitz.com/blog/accent-marks-spanish

- *How to Properly Use Spanish Intonation*
  https://www.spanish.academy/blog/how-to-properly-
  use-spanish-intonation/

- *15 Top Strategies for Teaching Adult Learners [+ FAQs]*
  https://pce.sandiego.edu/15-top-strategies-for-teaching-
  adult-learners-faqs/

- *Learn Spanish Grammar at StudySpanish.com*
  https://studyspanish.com/grammar

- *43 Fun Spanish Activities and Games for Grammar ...*
  https://www.fluentu.com/blog/educator-
  spanish/spanish-classroom-games/

- *Common Challenges When Learning Spanish as a ...*
  https://perfectsunsetschool.com/common-challenges-
  when-learning-spanish-as-a-foreign/

- *Language Learning for Adults: 5 Strategies to Make It Easier*
  https://languageadvantage.ca/language-learning-for-adults-5-strategies-to-make-it-easier/

- *Spain - Language, Culture, Customs and Etiquette*
  https://www.commisceo-global.com/resources/country-guides/spain-guide

- *101 Common Spanish Phrases You Need to Know*
  https://www.fluentin3months.com/common-spanish-phrases/

- *OnlineFreeSpanish: Study Spanish for free* at
  https://www.onlinefreespanish.com/

- *Teaching Spanish to Adults: Sharing Insights*
  https://drsaraheaton.wordpress.com/2011/03/11/teaching-spanish-to-adults-sharing-insights/

- *71 Common Spanish Phrases to Survive Any Conversation!*
  https://storylearning.com/learn/spanish/spanish-tips/common-spanish-phrases

- *Learn and practice Spanish for free! | TODO-CLARO.COM*
  https://www.todo-claro.com/e_index.php

- *Cultural immersion for learners of Spanish in Madrid*
  https://www.tildemadrid.com/cultural-immersion.html

- *15 Top Strategies for Teaching Adult Learners [+ FAQs]*
  https://pce.sandiego.edu/15-top-strategies-for-teaching-adult-learners-faqs/

- *Preterite vs Imperfect in Spanish: Master the Differences, ...*
  https://www.fluentu.com/blog/spanish/spanish-preterite-and-imperfect/

- *50+ Common Spanish Irregular Verbs: A Beginner's Guide* https://blog.rosettastone.com/common-spanish-irregular-verbs/

- *Spanish Present SUBJUNCTIVE - Learn and PRACTICE* https://holaquepasa.com/spanish-present-subjunctive/

- *Teaching Spanish to Adults: Sharing Insights* https://drsaraheaton.wordpress.com/2011/03/11/teaching-spanish-to-adults-sharing-insights/

- *50 Spanish Idioms To Use in Your Everyday Conversations* https://www.spanish.academy/blog/spanish-idioms/

- *Spanish Culture - Etiquette* https://culturalatlas.sbs.com.au/spanish-culture/spanish-culture-etiquette

- *Spain - Festivals, Holidays, Traditions* https://www.britannica.com/place/Spain/Festivals-and-holidays

- *11 Best Apps to Learn Spanish in 2023 [+Infographics]* https://letsspeakspanish.com/blog/learn-spanish-apps/

- *Can You Really Learn Spanish Through Movies and Music?* https://romancelanguagecentre.com/can-you-really-learn-spanish-through-movies-and-music/#:~:text=Listening%20to%20music%20and%20watching,that%20you%20must%20pick%20up.

- *The 6 Best Sites and Apps for Finding Spanish Conversation Partners* https://www.learnspanishconsalsa.com/6-best-sites-apps-finding-spanish-conversation-partners/

- *Improve Your Language Skills by Journaling in a Foreign ...* https://medium.com/an-idea/how-to-improve-your-language-skills-by-journaling-in-a-foreign-language-707d0c6b3563

- *7 Simple Steps to Create a Powerful Active Listening Practice* https://www.lucalampariello.com/powerful-active-listening-practice/

- *Enhancing Critical Thinking In Foreign Language Learners*https://www.sciencedirect.com/science/article/pii/S1877042811026759

- *25 Creative Writing Prompts to Practice Spanish* https://takelessons.com/blog/25-spanish-writing-prompts

- *6 Winning Public Speaking Tips For Non-Native English Speakers* https://www.inc.com/maya-hu-chan/6-winning-public-speaking-tips-for-non-native-english-speakers.html

- *The 10 Best Language Exchange Sites* https://www.linguasorb.com/blog/10-best-language-exchange-sites

- *Service-Learning Benefits for English Language Learners* https://files.eric.ed.gov/fulltext/EJ1241657.pdf

- *8 Professional Networks for Latina Professionals/Entrepreneurs* https://www.score.org/resource/blog-post/8-professional-networks-latina-professionals-or-entrepreneurs

Made in the USA
Las Vegas, NV
18 October 2024

97046511R00164